HISTORICAL ST. ANDREWS (Middle Ages Period).

1. Abbey Walk, 14th and 16th Cent.
2. Tiends Yett, for waggons.
3. Mill Port (machiolated bartizan).
4. Long Pier (Students' traditional walk).
5. Culdee Church, 1250.
6. Pends, 14th Cent.
7. St. Rule's Tower, 1127.
8. Cathedr__ __ded 1160.
9. Castle, _____ ___00
   Bottle _____ _____w_
0. Queen _____
1. St. Le_____
   On si_____
2. Novi_____
3. Dea_____
4. Lon_____
5. Old_____

16. St. Mary's College, 1537.
17. Queen Mary's Thorn, 1565.
18. Queen Mary's Thorn, 1565.
19. Holm Oak, c. 1750.
20. Holy Trinity Church, 1412.
21. Knights Templar property.
22. Mercat Cross—scene of numerous
    burnings and hangings.
23. St. Salvator's College Steeple, 1450.
24. Admirable Crichton's House, 1450
    (former Students' Union).
25. Blackfriars Chapel, 1525.
    ___st Port, re-built 1589.
    ___e Stane, legendary.
    ___ch Lake and Witch Hill (Witches
    ___ned till 18th Cent.).
    ___w Butts, used for archery until 1754.
    ___d Course, birthplace of golf.
    ___oundel Tower.

First printed 1973

Printed by J. & G. Innes, Ltd.,
at Edenside Printing Works,
Cupar, Fife,
Scotland.

DEDICATION

To F. M. B.

ABOUT ST. ANDREWS
—AND ABOUT

By JAMES K. ROBERTSON

Jacket Designs by J. Putter, D.A. Des. (Edin.)
St. Andrews

"CITIZEN OFFICE ", ST. ANDREWS
FIFE, SCOTLAND

A

ACKNOWLEDGMENTS

For the portrait of the past contained in these pages I acknowledge gratefully my debt to historians such as C. J. Lyon, Maitland Anderson, D. Hay Fleming, Connelly, Wood, E. S. Robertson, Russell Kirk and R. G. Cant. Also the University authorities for their co-operation and help ; the Librarian and staff of the University Library for placing material at my disposal ; Peter Adamson, University Photographer, for many fine illustrations.

To all of these, and many others of Town and Gown, for their encouragement and active assistance, I am deeply grateful.

J. K. ROBERTSON.

South Street,
St. Andrews.
April, 1973.

FOREWORD

THE Royal Burgh of St. Andrews can claim to be historically the most prominent of the Scottish Small Burghs that ceased to exist in all but name on the implementation of regionalised administration.

Only the Church of Scotland ecclesiastical boundaries that mark its parishes now remain to delineate the nation's former ecclesiastical capital ; the brightest jewel in the crown of the old Kingdom of Fife. But, of a certainty, of its unique individuality and heritage this old grey city can never be shorn. So much of Scotland's history has happened within its gates over the centuries.

St. Andrews came first into prominence when pilgrims were attracted in large numbers in the 8th and 9th Centuries by the miraculous powers that were being attributed to relics of the Apostle St. Andrew which were enshrined in the little township. The religious importance of the town waxed as the number of these devout and earnest pilgrims grew. St. Andrews, thanks to the ambition and pride of the Church, became a jewel with an absorbing story of many facets ; often a bloody story. It reached the zenith of its lustre in the early 16th Century when not only was it one of the chief trading cities in the realm, but its bishop was the Primate of Scotland. Its importance as a shrine of pilgrimage was the prime root of its prosperity and fame. That fame and prosperity waxed through the Middle Ages up to the post-Reformation years. The Reformation was by far the most important single event in the city's history, since the ousting of Catholicism had more affect on St. Andrews than anywhere else in Britain. With the loss of its ecclesiastic significance, its prosperity waned to a critical degree. Then came the dramatic nineteenth century revival.

The douce and dignified family resort of to-day is once again a shrine and a mecca of pilgrims . . . the Mecca of Golf. A game has brought to it centuries later a new fame and a fresh prosperity.

A placid atmosphere in to-day's streets belies the turbulence of its history, except when the city's venerable Old Course transforms into a modern jousting arena of some international golf event. Fine university buildings, old and new, contribute handsomely in conferring an air of solid dignity. They also provide ideal meeting places for international events of another character ; the conferences, symposia and varied gatherings of the academic world.

Stern guardian cliffs have long ceased to serve any purpose of fortification. Now they are a stalking ground for naturalists and a haunt of marine biologists ; the viewing platform also of a majestic panorama for tourists.

Understandably, because of its visitors attracted by the lure of golf and by the prestige of its university, St. Andrews is a cosmopolitan little community. Summer and winter, it is well accustomed to foreign garb and strange tongues. The citizens are urbane and natively polite. With a quiet pride in their ancient heritage which they preserve with loving care, they are not lacking in the traditional business acumen of the Scot. This they reveal in the quality and service of their shops. It could be a quality inherited from their trading ancestors of ten centuries ago. These were already well accustomed to welcome to their mediaeval Senzie Fair a cosmopolitan stream of merchants from faraway Europe. To-day, the tongues in the streets are even more polyglot.

Already the city claims to itself an impressive bibliography, with many volumes that have been devoted exclusively to one or other individual aspect of its glittering and multi-sided history.

But St. Andrews means many things to many people to-day ; it is more than merely a museum of the past as represented by romantic-looking ruins. The little city lays claim to key importance and interest in a number of spheres. The intention in this volume is to draw a portrait that encompasses these manifold interests ; to depict St. Andrews as a composite whole in which to-day ranks in importance equally with yesterday.

Such a portrait now has a timely purpose. It seeks to make an appraisal of St. Andrews up to its assimilation into Regional government ; to remind the world of its many present-day features and attractions ; to recall also its storied past and its heritage from that past ; to tell of its university to-day and yesterday and to recall to mind the unique niche it occupies as the Home of Golf.

St. Andrews has played a key part in Scotland's history. Its name is quintessential of Scotland, as it will always remain.

J. K. R.

CONTENTS

LIST OF ILLUSTRATIONS

STORY OF A BURGH

*" A grand place, St. Andrews.   You have there the
essence of all the antiquity of Scotland, in good
clean condition "*

(Thomas Carlyle)

A CERTAIN few people there are who are destined to lead lives that
become sated with the whole gamut of human emotions ; who attract
extremes of tragedy and joy ; of love and hate ; In the same way it is
the destiny of some places to become a backcloth for violent and
turbulent scenes that punctuate the course of their histories.

Such a place is St. Andrews, ancient capital of the Kingdom of
Fife.

Originally a hamlet of fishers existing hand-to-mouth around the
estuary of the Kinness Burn, the rivulet that empties placidly at the
harbour into the North Sea, it became in the eighth century a place of
religious note.   In the succeeding centuries this tiny hamlet developed,
to become in time the most powerful and stimulating city in Scotland,
and the nation's ecclesiastical capital.   Splendid scenes and historic
events were enacted within its gates ; terrible deeds of cruelty came to
be witnessed on its streets ; acts that were born of bigotry, superstition and political machinations.   Indescribably revolting per-
petrations were committed in the name of holy religion that included
burnings at the stake and gloating tortures of men and women.

Within sight and sound of such deeds arose Scotland's earliest
seat of learning.   The University of St. Andrews was founded in
1413, thanks to ecclesiastical influence and initiative.   The University
has not always remained academically sequestered and aloof from
events around it.   Its masters have ever, in the course of its own
eventful history, jealously guarded the original aims and pursuits of
their university no less than the privileges that were granted to it on
its foundation.

Nearby, just outside the mediaeval gates, the citizens, masters
and students, along with proud priests, ambitious soldiers and
haughty nobles, all found pleasure in a simple game that they played

1

with a ball and stick. The pastime evolved down the centuries into the sport of golf which has swept the world and brought a new fame to St. Andrews.

In the sunshine of a quiet summer or autumn day when the sky is limpid blue and the atmosphere incredibly clear ; as rippling wavelets gently lap on golden sands, it could seem that time has erased totally the memory of man's inhumanity to man in the cause of Christianity that once darkened the name of this placid old city of to-day.

But there are other days when the town is the old, grey city of Andrew Lang, the 19th Century student poet and historian. Then the uneasy emanations of a sickly aura of singeing flesh and of blood and broken bones creeps chill and unbidden into the receptive mind. A chilling aspect is sensed in the skeletal outline of the cathedral's brooding ruins ; a menace in the stillness of the Pends and in the sullen shadow of claustrophobic Priory walls.

To slip off from the bustle and stir of a cheerful and busy South Street, and stand within the midst of those ruins, two minutes' walk away, can instantly transport the receptive mind through time into the world of an earlier and darker age.

To-day we find a unique burgh of some 11,000 inhabitants expanding at a recently accelerated pace. University students add some 3,000 to its populace for eight months of the year . . . a number that has been planned for further increase. At summer's height the basic community is trebled by tourists from many parts of the world.

The visitor looks first at the hotels and other accommodation that the city provides for his convenience and comfort. He will find them an ample number in quantity as befits a thriving holiday resort. They range from the comfortable to the luxurious in quality, and, in one instance at least, to the bizarre in architecture, an exception to the solid ashlar buildings that distinguish the town. That architectural deviation provides no criterion of the top rating of its accommodation and cuisine. ' Well, they brought a stranger to design it ' is how the citizens dismiss a building which never fails to evoke comment.

The shops in this old, grey city that prides itself on its well-preserved antiquity, will possibly surprise and gratify with their modern presentation in the ancient surroundings, and with the unvarying friendliness and courteous service given.

Probably next to come under the scrutiny of questing tourist eyes will be the buildings lining the broad sweep of the old city's clean main streets, and the snug narrowness of ancient pends and wynds. The visitor will note buildings that have withstood the ravages of centuries in remarkable degree. Many of them are wonderfully preserved as, for instance, the fine sixteenth and seventeenth century town houses of South Street, the restored houses of Dean's Court and the neighbouring Roundel, both late sixteenth century. Most of all, the classical outline of the Collegiate Church of St. Salvator in North Street that goes back to the 1400s. And at every turn of the head there are to be encountered the early twelfth century ruins of the once-magnificent Cathedral. They loom starkly impressive to form a romantic silhouette on the eastern skyline.

The Castle, battered by cannon and by the incessant North Sea storms, stands within close view of the Cathedral and of the adjoining tower of St. Rule. A puzzle to antiquarians, this tower, ascetically trim, is ascribed to be no later than early twelfth century. The sturdy beauty of the renovated Town Church enriches the wide vista of South Street, a spaciously handsome thoroughfare that is adorned with a wealth of architectural gems.

A simple study reveals the lay-out of the city's three main streets as representing functional planning based on the primitive dictates of self-preservation and of geography. This layout was undoubtedly conceived as part of the ambitious religious planning that intended the Cathedral of St. Andrew to become the finest and greatest in Scotland ; to rival the best in Christendom in beauty and impressiveness. Those three approach avenues to the Cathedral comprise the earliest and the finest example of ancient town-planning in Britain. The centre of the old city that evolved subsequently remains over a thousand years later the essential township then created. The thoroughfares of South Street, Market Street and North Street, still spacious to-day, are linked by narrow wynds, and lead inexorably seawards to the Cathedral and Priory, the hub of mediaeval St. Andrews, thence to the tip of the cliff-girt headland that thrusts defiantly out into the grey North Sea.

An exploration of these streets reveals innumerable tangible links with long-past centuries ; such links are visible in the thousand-year old yew tree that still shades a South Street garden ; in the mediaeval Scottish ' long riggs ' or narrow gardens of Middle Age mansion houses. They emphasize the venerable age of the mystery tower of

St. Rule and of the vanished Priory's massive walls that still encircle the lost lands of what was once a rich and expansive ecclesiastical precinct.

A happy combination of evolutionary factors transformed the first Christians of the area, the primitive Culdee community of upwards of a thousand years ago, into the internationally-known St. Andrews of to-day that is fairly described as the most famous place of its size in the world. The radial point of the city of the present is no longer the Cathedral ; that point has shifted towards its western tip ; to the first tee of the Old Course from which the wide prominence of St. Andrews to-day so largely derives. The origins of golf are, like some other features of the city, shrouded by the curtains of time. The life of St. Andrews still centres largely on its golf links (p. 109).

Aware of the prestige of the little city in one or other, if not all of the three spheres of its influence, the visitor would be entitled to expect a much larger place in terms of population than is the case.

But this Scottish small burgh that was once a cathedral city did become at one time one of the largest cities in Scotland as well as being the most important ; its bishop was Primate of the nation's Church.

Present-day statistics hold no relevance in assessing the importance of this place that provides a direct link with the days of five centuries ago. The antiquarian is happy to walk the streets of the old town and be transported back to mediaeval days ; the scholar to stroll within the cloistered portals of an ancient university that has a significant place in modern science. The golfer alone may be obsessedly concerned with figures ; but only to the extent of those representing the tally of his latest 18 holes of the Old Course . . . the oldest golf course.

Climate, naturally is of moment to all tourists. They will nod approval of an annual rainfall of just under 28 inches ; sunshine above the average for our northerly latitudes, and a tang of ozone as exhilarating as champagne.

Such is the colourful backcloth on which to investigate modern St. Andrews . . . the backcloth that time's loom has woven within the framework of a lengthy existence—a framework of history, learning and of golf.

4

THE LEGENDS

" *Tis thought when St. Regulus landed,*
The bones of St. Andrew he bore."

(*Scott*)

LEGEND and fact are intermingled in the story of how the tiny, pre-historic community that existed around the mouth of the Kinness rivulet came to bear the name of St. Andrews.

The legend itself has two derivations differing slightly in origin and fancy. They unite in the common object of glorifying the omni-potence of the Church. In one, Fordun, the early historian, writes of a Greek monk, Regulus or Rule, who was abbot of the monastery of Patras, and guardian of the relics of St. Andrew, the apostle. Regulus was directed in a vision to abandon his country and to leave for a distant land . . . an island in a great ocean of the name of Albion. But first, ran the saga, he must visit the shrine of the Apostle Andrew, whose relics lay in Patras, and take from the tomb certain bones. The saint eventually did so, and " accompanied by seventeen other monks and three nuns ", set sail. After two years of storm-tossed voyaging they were shipwrecked in St. Andrews Bay . . . a fate that has overtaken hundreds of vessels since. They escaped with their lives, and with the relics. The evangelists found themselves in a heavily-wooded country infested by wild boars of huge size and fer-ocity. The land, in the language of the inhabitant Picts, was Muckros, the promontory of the boars. This was said to be about A.D. 390. The Pictish chief, Hergist or Angus, welcomed them hos-pitably and soon became, with his tribe, a convert from druidical worship to Christianity.

Angus presented the missionaries with a large tract of land at the place where they landed, and on the tip of the promontory he erected for them a church where in time the relics of St. Andrew they brought with them formed a miraculous shrine.

The foundations of the ancient church of St. Mary-on-the-Crag built by the Kaledei, or Culdees, as this religious settlement became known, are clearly traced at the top of the path leading down from the headland to the harbour pier.

5

Soon after, Angus changed the name of Muckros to Kilrymount, the King's Mount.   This name continued until the mid-ninth century when Kenneth Macalpin, King of the Scots, conquered the Picts and transferred his palace from Abernethy, twenty miles west, to Kilrymont with its expanding church.   The place came to be known in turn as St. Andrews because of the miraculous powers that were increasingly coming to be attributed to the relics of the saint enshrined there . . . . an ancient Lourdes !

On the other hand the Augustinian monks, founders of the Priory in 1124, shortly after work had begun on the cathedral, set the legend later.   Their story also contains certain facts as well as fantasy. According to them, Ungus or Angus, King of the Picts, was camped in Berwickshire and about to be attacked by a large army.   He ' saw a blinding light and heard the voice of St. Andrew bidding him attack, headed by the cross of Christ '.   He was directed that afterwards he must dedicate a tenth of his wealth to God and St. Andrew.   Angus was victorious and on his return was met by the monk named Raigail or Regulus at the summit of Kilrymont who had just arrived, bearing relics of St. Andrew.

Angus gave that place to God and St. Andrew.

A possibility suggested by some historians but not clearly established, could be that Cainnich, or Kenneth, a missionary of the Irish Christian colleges that produced Columba, came to Kilrymont and founded a church there.   When he returned to Ireland he left in charge Regulus who had accompanied him.   To Kenneth's teaching gathered as eager pupils the Culdees—the Cultores Dei or Kaledei— and they remained known by that name long after their Order had disappeared elsewhere in Scotland.   The church of St. Mary on the Rock which they built, continued as a separate place of worship from the much later edifice erected by approval of King David First's reorganised Roman Church, and it survived until the Reformation.   At one time a chapel royal, the Culdee Church saw its prestige and influence systematically undermined as the Order was superseded by the Catholics of Rome who had David's special protection.

The legend that Regulus or Rule was a Greek saint who came to St. Andrews from Patras with relics of Saint Andrew by open boat must, of course, be regarded as a story wholly fictitious, built upon only a tenuous basis, although the saint's supposed flight from Patras and the appearance of the relics in St. Andrews do synchronise in time. A cave hidden by an overhanging cliff between the pier and the Castle is the legendary hermit shelter of St. Rule, from which he is said to have first preached in the area of the Boars' headland.

Established is the historical fact that somewhere between 732 and 761 Bishop Acca fled north from Hexham for sanctuary, with a great treasure which included certain relics of St. Andrew. It is not explained how he got them from Constantinople where they were enshrined, but relics there were, and they were revered as authentic. The Culdees became their guardians. Acca was well received, and he was soon able to build a new church on the headland which he felt constrained to name after St. Andrew as his own church at Hexham, destroyed by Norsemen, had been dedicated to that apostle. The relics as the years progressed came to be accredited with miraculous powers, and pilgrims arrived from far and wide in increasing numbers to worship there. As the fame of Kilrymont spread, additional privileges were granted to the Culdee community by the Pictish and then by the Scottish kings who conquered and succeeded them. Its religious celebrity continued to expand to the extent that St. Andrew the Apostle was constituted patron saint of all Scotland ! There is little doubt, as Sir Steven Runciman suggests, that the main purpose of the legends was to glorify the See of St. Andrews and to justify it in its primacy within the Scottish Church.

So the township grew as the reorganised Scottish Church, under Roman dominance, deliberately exploited this saintly prestige to make it the ecclesiastical centre and stronghold of Scotland. So, too the bishops of the St. Andrews See became in fact, and later in name, the primates of the nation. The ultimate seal of ecclesiastical splendour was at last conferred in 1472 when St. Andrews was elevated as Metropolitan See of Scotland.

No narration of legends surrounding St. Andrews is complete without mention being made of possibly the most ancient relic yet the least known in its possession—the Blue Stane. This comes down in the annals as having been a stone altar of pagan times. It was used for long as a meeting or trysting place, and was regarded with superstitious awe by passers-by. Men would give it a placatory pat and women a cautious curtsey in the way-going. It is said that the pikemen of St. Andrews touched it as assurance before departing in 1314 for Bannockburn. The curious will find it hidden by shrubbery in the garden of the Station Hotel in Alexandra Place, which is in the vicinity of the conspicuous Hope Park Church.

A MAGNIFICENT FAILURE

" To pace our lost Cathedral's grass-grown floor
Through skeleton walls and altars overthrown."

(*J. C. Shairp*)

How the city of to-day evolved from the tiny Pictish community of
distant ages in the slow spread of Christianity is itself a fascinating
story.   The nucleus of that history is written in the ruins clustered
around the headland's tip.

To the little community of fisher folk of Kilrymont came the
Columban missionaries whose Culdees founded the Celtic Church.
Their Kilrymont church was St. Mary-on-the-Crag (1250), its foundations traced out, just outside the walls of the later Cathedral, and, as
stated, overlooking the harbour.   A rock at the harbour entrance is
still named the Lady Craig and legend has it that the first-ever church
in the area, a makeshift erection, was built on that rock by the ascetic
Culdees, but was later abandoned in favour of the prominent headland site.

The historical significance attaching to the outlined foundations
on the Kirkhill, or the Kirk Heugh, to give it its early name, is considerable.   Legend apart, and the existence of previous churches or
hermitages of Culdee missionaries is confirmed in varying versions of
the legends, the church of the Kirkhill, overlooking the magnificence
of St. Andrews Bay, was undoubtedly one of the earliest of the Celtic
churches in Scotland—a relic of the beginnings of Christianity in this
country.

It was the misfortune of the Culdees, after some three centuries
of fostering Christianity in this wild part of Scotland, that they should
find little favour with David I.   He infused much of the Saxon element
into the Scottish Church and opened the way to the ascendancy of the
Roman form of worship.   In his reign the Culdees were overshad-
owed and supplanted by the institution of the Chapter of Canons
Regular and the Royal preference given to them.   Soon they were
deprived of many of their possessions and privileges, but still managed a century later to retain their chief prerogative of taking part in
the election of a bishop.   For almost another hundred years they

9

resisted the surrender of that privilege. By the middle of the thirteenth century this Culdee establishment was presided over by a Provost and it is therefore one of the earliest provostries or collegiate churches in the kingdom. In that century it was elevated to a Chapel Royal—a privilege and importance that it retained for some two hundred years. Not until 1606 was it made over by statute to the episcopal archbishopric which James I tried to set up. The chapel had been one of the buildings that was damaged at the Reformation and thereafter it quickly became a deserted ruin. Important discoveries were made during ' diggings ' in 1860 when a part of the Kirkhill was being levelled for the installation of a gun battery. These finds to-day form a prominent part of the Cathedral museum exhibits as a direct link with the Celtic era of Kilrymont.

The Kirkhill Church, of course, for long contained the holy relics of the Apostle Andrew on which its fame was built. They attracted religious pilgrims from an ever-widening area to the expanding city. A hospice had to be built to accommodate these pilgrims at nearby St. Nicholas, which later was to become a leper colony. The dread disease was, no doubt, one of the unwelcome ' gifts ' conveyed thither by pilgrims hoping for miraculous cure.

When King David re-organised the Scottish Church on Roman lines to replace the traditional Celtic structure founded by the Columban missionaries, the succeeding bishops and archbishops of the See became overlords of the community of St. Andrews. The deliberations and actions of its civic rulers were made subject to ecclesiastical control. Although the city held fifth place among ten burghs incorporated by David into Royal burghs, the Church retained for itself some of the most valuable privileges conveyed by the charter.

David appointed Turgot first bishop of the See and that ambitious prelate quickly capitalised deliberately on the town's religious fame by promoting it as the ecclesiastical stronghold of Scotland. He proceeded, in pursuance of his plan, to build several fine churches throughout the country and all were brought within his See. His erections included the first town church, Holy Trinity, which he built conspicuously in the centre of the headland directly overlooking the Bay to the north and east ; it stood on the site that was later to be occupied by the much more imposing cathedral. The impressive Church of the Holy Trinity standing on the present site in South Street is a much later work (p. 91). Queen Margaret, the Maid of

Norway, also did much to encourage the spread of Roman Catholicism. A woman of enlightenment, among many other things she succeeded in doing for her subjects, according to Turgot, her admiring biographer, was to break up the Scots habit of selling their wives !

In pursuance of Turgot's policy, Bishop Arnold, his successor, in the presence of King Malcolm Fifth, laid the foundations in 1159 of the cathedral. It was a church of magnificent concept, but it has to be conceded that it turned out to be, in fact, an architectural failure . . . an ill-starred failure. Ten succeeding prelates over the next 160 years contributed money and labour to promote the lavish erection. The cathedral reached the stage of consecration by 1318 and a magnificent ceremony was conducted by Bishop Lamberton in the presence of Robert the Bruce, that renowned of Scottish heroes, supported by the whole of the Church and peerage. The gathering included seven bishops, fifteen abbots and almost every earl and other member of Scotland's nobility remaining after the wreck of revolution and war that was ended by Bruce's unification.

THE VANISHED RELICS

From inception to completion the cathedral remained in use for almost exactly four centuries during which time it developed numerous flaws in construction, largely because the ambitions of its architects outran their engineering skill. Even before the upheaval of the Reformation whose supporters were wrongly accused of its destruction, it had become unusable having already been crumbling for many years to an accelerating decay. Dr. Hay Fleming, the St. Andrews antiquarian, gives a detailed account of the progress of the work and of the numerous obstacles to its erection down the years, in his ' Researches '. He claims also that by 1303 the relics of St. Andrew had been removed from the Chapel Royal on the Kirkheugh, and had become the most important and most prized of the Cathedral treasures. On the other hand, some historians believe that the Culdees, foreseeing such an eventuality, forestalled Roman action by removing them to their Monastery of St. Serf on Loch Leven.

Whatever their fate, the relics vanished, but when and where ?

The chief architect during the lengthy building of the Cathedral was William Malvoisin. He succeeded Bishop Robert who was too harassed with buttressing the Castle to be in a position to devote much

11

time or money to the church. Malvoisin during the whole of his long episcopate in succession to Robert, pushed on the work, and it was also prosecuted eagerly by his own successors, David de Bernham and Gameline. Wynton, the ryhming historian, credits Bishop William Wishart (1271), with the completion of the nave where, in fact, the architectural style changes from the semi-circular to the pointed. From the existing remains, Hay Fleming suggests, it might have been conjectured that the chancel had been projected across the transepts and into the nave, so as to include its first bay. In support, Wynton's further description exactly tallies with this, for he speaks of Wishart's addition as beginning at the third pillar from the chancel door. Wishart also roofed what he built and also erected the west gable of the Cathedral.

Times of stress followed for the progress of the incomplete Cathedral building. Part of the fabric was ruined in a storm and the canons of the Priory despite their wealth, ran out of money. Then followed the desolating Wars of Succession and it was not until the year 1318 that the Cathedral was sufficiently advanced to be consecrated and used.

Rather ironically in retrospect, Edward I of England, ' the Hammer of the Scots,' and his queen each offered a golden ouch to the arm bone of St. Andrew preserved then in the Cathedral. This in March, 1303. In July of the following year Edward had caused twenty-two wagon loads of lead to be stripped from the roofs of the Cathedral and the Priory for the use of the engines with which he was then besieging Stirling Castle. He afterwards paid the Prior and convent for this lead and permitted them to receive twenty oaks fit for timber from the forest of Clackmannan to repair the Priory properties.

Succeeding bishops and priors found steady outlet for surplus revenues in embellishing the Cathedral further, but misfortune constantly dogged the project. A disastrous fire in 1378 was responsible for a great deal of the work of past years having to be done over again. During this period the demands of the Church to create a cathedral unequalled in Britain in opulence and magnificence were insatiable. Money and work were lavished on it in adornment and furnishings that made it a target in later and less respectful times for plunder by all and sundry.

Relics of the fire of 1378 were discovered at the beginning of this century in the form of hundreds of pieces of shattered stained glass

12

and fused lead-framings which had been buried for centuries in debris. All showed traces of tremendous heat. Numerous fragments of richly-sculptured stones have also been discovered from time to time around the foundations, many of them of the Celtic Church period. They apparently, had been deliberately broken up, and used as ordinary building material on the Cathedral by succeeding generations of stone masons—a point emphasized by Dr. Johnson following his famous visit of 1773. This, to some extent became the fate of large parts of the Cathedral itself in its own early stages of decay. Much of its stonework was simply annexed as common property and was cannibalised into many local houses and properties. By no means inconceivable is the possibility that there are stones in existing buildings which came successively from the Culdee Church and then the Cathedral !

The fire was not the last of the catalogue of misfortunes that befell this monument to ecclesiastical pride and pomp. For example, the gable of the south transept was badly damaged in 1409 by an unusually fierce storm.

Although John Knox's inflammatory sermon on the eve of the Reformation was believed by many to have inspired the final destruction of the Cathedral, several authorities have emphasized that the real cause was inept architecture that gave rise to structural faults and decay, allied to later neglect. It is true that at the Reformation the church was ' stripped of its imagery and symbols ', but the fabric was relatively unharmed for the simple reason that it was already verging on ruins.

Some historians appear to have allowed their imaginations to run riot in recording the events of that frenzied time. Professor Tennant, writing of ' the dinging doon of the Cathedral ', related how—

> " The cappar roofs that dazzlit heaven
> Were frae their rafters rent and riven ".

The truth was that there never were copper roofs to be rent ! They were a figment of poetic imagination, strangely untypical of academic accuracy.

It is important, therefore, to record that not a single scrap of contemporary evidence exists to prove that the Cathedral was demolished, let alone severely damaged, at the Reformation. A Catholic historian, Bishop Lesley, confirms this when he wrote only

13

that the images of all the kirks in the town were burned ; and that the monasteries of the Friars, the Chapel of the Kirkhill and ' all uther privat chapels within the toun ' were pulled down.   Had the damage been more extensive he would not have failed to record and emphasize it.

Within the past century a number of archaeologists have contributed many discoveries during work within the cathedral confines and these have subsequently been collated and added to by the Ministry of Works.   That body since 1936 has taken over the precincts, and improved and preserved the fabric in its usual admirable manner.

UNSOLVED MYSTERY

There remains, arising out of all this, the unsolved mystery of St. Andrews that has defied the efforts of treasure hunters and of historians, namely, failure to elicit the fate of the Cathedral's priceless treasures, and particularly of the relics of the Apostle Andrew, after the Reformation.   Although they had long lost their mystic appeal and had become little more than religious curios, the relics still ranked beyond price for their historical significance, and the link they would have provided with the city's beginnings.   And where were the innumerable costly gifts donated down the centuries ?

Kirk, the American historian, suggests that ' perhaps the rabble that followed John Knox from Crail after his historic Reformation sermon, flung the relics in their casket into the sea, or burnt them ' !

No doubt a great deal of treasure was plundered at that time by the avaricious mobs, and Kirk's speculation represents more than just a possibility.   The destruction of hagiological relics and symbols was invariably the first act perpetrated by frenzied religious mobs in order to vent their public hatred of all that smacked of popery (p. 82).

Along with the relics of St. Andrew—the sacred bones—many valuable treasures of the Cathedral vanished without trace, although some may have been secreted out of St. Andrews, as the clouds of the impending storm from the south-east gathered ominously.   One of the local weather sayings is that nothing good comes out of Crail, meaning the south-easterly wind.   The Reformation storm came to St. Andrews on the wings of Knox's sermon, ' out of Crail '.

Whither the relics vanished is an intriguing mystery many have tried to solve, but it is one that is unlikely ever to be answered now other than in vague theories and speculations.

14

Charles I in 1634 proposed to restore the Cathedral, but it was soon found that its fabric had been despoiled so much in the intervening years of neglect, as to be deemed beyond repair. Lead, timber and in particular, stonework, had all been removed. The buildings had been treated as an open quarry. There are subsequent buildings proudly standing still in St. Andrews some of whose stonework is Cathedral fabric. In 1826 the huge accumulation of centuries of debris was removed and the vast Cathedral floor and pillar bases were laid bare. This was in addition to the stained glass discovered from the 1378 fire. The clearance and sifting led to the uncovering of stone coffins and later to the restoration of the ruins to their present-day appearance. In the Cathedral museum there is on view a magnificent collection of Celtic pottery and mediaeval monuments, unrivalled in Scotland. It also contains other pottery, glasswork and relics discovered on the site.

Nearby St. Rule Tower has remained an unsolved mystery to antiquarians and architects and satisfactory answers to their probings are unlikely now. Some placed its erection as early as the fourth century, but this assessment was subsequently discredited. Generally, Bishop Robert is believed to have built it around 1140. As the first church of the post-Culdee period it is by far the most interesting of the Romanesque churches in Scotland. An old beam in the first landing of the ' Square Tower ', as it is generally known, is affirmed to be a timber from one of the wrecked Armada vessels that strewed the coasts, thriftily used for repair purposes. Unlike the more pretentious Cathedral, the Tower's architecture has triumphantly withstood the ravages of the years, and it still stands foursquare to the winds, a challenge, and one of the most intriguing of St. Andrews many mysteries. (Admission to the Cathedral and to St. Rule's Tower is regulated by the Ministry of Works).

King David I was a deeply pious Scottish monarch noted, as mentioned, for his liberality to the Church. During his reign it was due to his munificence that the great Augustinian Priory of St. Andrews was begun, the bulwark of early prosperity. The massive walls, erected much later to surround the whole Priory and Cathedral precincts, are now all that remain, dominating still the old town as they always have done, by their venerable and still massive strength !

The Priory was destined to flourish from its institution in 1144. It was magnificently endowed by succeeding kings and nobles, until it owned extensive lands throughout the country. Its priors ranked next to the bishop himself in power. King Alexander presented the tract of hunting country to the south of the town, running from Dunino in the east to Dairsie in the west, which was at that time for obvious reasons described as ' The Boar's Chase '. The tusks of a giant boar are incorporated into the old arms of the city ; the original tusks, it is chronicled, were for long suspended by silver chains in the Priory cloister and they endured well into the sixteenth century.

Under the patronage of the all-powerful Roman Church, St. Andrews in the wake of its Priory, flourished and prospered. It continued to prosper for four centuries until the Reformation brought about the most dramatic change in the city's history. John Knox set the flames alight in Scotland with his defiant sermons in Crail and St. Andrews. This widespread religious revolution throughout Europe that broke the domination of Catholicism in Scotland, had an immediate and calamitous effect on its capital city.

The influence of St. Andrews which had reached its peak at the beginning of the 1500s, when it was a city of some 14,000 inhabitants, quickly evaporated. There followed almost a hundred years when, caught up in the struggle for power by the Crown and the Episcopalian Church on the one side, and the Reformers on the other, the city's fortunes swayed in a precarious balance. A see-saw of political manoeuvrings followed, and for a short spell episcopacy restored to St. Andrews its former ecclesiastical eminence, but its power proved only fleeting. The end of the city's ecclesiastical influence and prestige was close, but was preceded by a bewildering see-saw of events that followed in the wake of the Stuart attempts to establish the English faith.

At this period, 1605, the episcopal Archbishop Gladstanes, who later reviewed and extended the prized privileges granted to the city in previous Royal charters, was appointed also to the Chancellorship of the University.

A special Royal interest in the city, stimulated undoubtedly by Gladstanes, who enjoyed his King's special favour, was shown by James VI then and in the period up to the time when he paid a visit twelve years later. So, for a delusory spell the balance of spiritual power swayed again full span in favour of the city—the centre now of Scottish Episcopalianism.

But by 1638, a bare twenty years on, the Episcopal regime, like the Catholic before it, had again fallen, although it was by no means finally destroyed. Much was still to happen. With the passing of still another decade came its temporary restoration through the persistence of the monarchy. St. Andrews was yet again for another brief period, the ecclesiastical centre of Scotland !

James Sharp, once Reform minister of Crail, was summoned to London and returned to Scotland with a large and armed retinue behind him. He returned also as the Episcopal Bishop of St. Andrews and Chancellor of its University, and imbued with all the frenetic zeal and enthusiasm of the apostate !

The glowing prospects the city merchants may have then visualised were quickly to be dispelled by subsequent events that introduced a pitiful period in the history of St. Andrews.

DECLINE AND FALL

" St. Andrews, they say that thy glories are gone,
That thy streets are deserted, thy castles o'erthrown "

(*G. F. Carnegie, 1830*)

IT was ecclesiastical demise, complete and final, that sealed the
seventeenth century fate of the declining city as the culmination
of a protracted see-saw of religious struggles.   The date of the
death blow when the Episcopal archbishopric was abolished was
1689.   The overthrow was hastened by the murder of Sharp in 1679
on Magus Muir by a band of Covenanters, and even more by
reprisals on the Covenanters of a sickening ferocity.   The situation
was in essence a repetition of the fall of Catholicism over a hundred
years earlier, with brutal repression succeeding only in breeding
revolt of an even greater ferocity.

The coach road from the south in those days ran through Magus,
an area of high moorland that lies some three miles west of
St. Andrews and a mile south of Strathkinness village.

Simple stone memorials commemorate each of three separate
terrible deeds perpetrated in the name of religion.   They stand at
Magus, some distance from the present road and in the vicinity of the
spot where Sharp was waylaid and killed.   Although little-known
and seldom visited, these monuments are important in the history of
St. Andrews as reminders of one of the most savage times in
Scotland's story.

James Sharp, because of his apostasy, was the most hated of the
Episcopal bishops in Scotland at the time.   He was on his way back
from Edinburgh when he was by chance waylaid by nine
Covenanters who were seeking another and lesser man.   All were
sworn adherents of the Solemn League and Covenant whose purpose
was to preserve Presbyterianism.   The band was led by David
Hackston of Rathillet, who apart from religion, held a private grudge
against the Archbishop.   They encountered him and on Magus a new
chapter in Scotland's bloody religious history was written.   Accompanied by his daughter, Sharp was within sight of the city when his
coach was stopped.   He was stabbed sixteen times by various

19

members of the band. All his papers, gold and money were taken, and his daughter barely escaped with her life when she frantically sought to intervene.

The death of Sharp heralded the climax of the notorious ' killing time ' when fanatacism and bigotry shamed Scotland of the period— a sorry time in its history.

At the funeral of the Archbishop which took place fourteen days later the chief exhibit in the mourning procession apart from that of the corpse, was ' the bloody gown in which His Grace was slain '. The fatal coach, with coachman, horses and postilions all clad in the sombre trappings of deepest mourning, were also there.

No sooner had Bishop Paterson (notorious as the inventor of the thumbscrews) preached the Archbishop's funeral sermon than a grim persecution of all known adherents of the Covenant began throughout the country. The penalty of association with or sheltering any of the field preachers or their audience was 20,000 merks. So loud was raised the Government hue and cry that Andrew Gullan of the parish of Balmerino, some fifteen miles distant, sought to disappear. Gullan had been present when the prelate was killed, though, like his more distinguished companion, Hackston, he had declined to take any active part in the hated tyrant's murder. He is said to have lingered some distance away with the horses and there is little doubt that it was Gullan who, when Sharp's daughter rushed between her father and his assailants, tried to give her protection from their flailing swords. This was confirmed at his trial, but did nothing to temper the inhuman cruelty of his punishment.

The notable point about Gullan is that of the nine men present when the Archbishop was murdered, the only two who did not take an actual part in the assassination, himself and Hackston, were the two who paid the penalty of their lives. Five other Covenanters were brought to Magus for retribution. All were survivors of the Battle of Bothwell Brig. They had no connection with the murder, but they had stubbornly refused to recant their faith.

It was also his fierce religious faith that brought about the discovery of Gullan and he was tried at Edinburgh for complicity in the Archbishop's death. He was quickly found guilty and was sentenced to mutilation and hanging at Edinburgh Gallowlee—his head to be hung on the Tolbooth at Cupar and his body exhibited in chains at Magus Muir. Gullan died, to the last denying that he was guilty of murder though he frankly admitted that he had been in company with ' those who executed justice upon a Judas who had sold the Kirk of Scotland for 51,000 merks a year.'

One of the three stones to be seen at Magus was erected in his memory. It stands in a small clump of trees a few yards to the west of Claremont Farm on the Craigtoun Road to Ceres. The inscription, almost indecipherable, reads :—

" The gravestone of Andrew Gullan who suffered at the Gallowlee of Edinburgh and afterwards was hung upon a pole, and lieth here. ''

> " A faithful martyr here doth lie ;
> A witness against perjury,
> Who cruelly was put to death
> To gratify proud prelate's wrath
> They cut his hands ere he was dead,
>   And after that struck off his head.
>   To Magus Muir they did him bring
>   His body on a pole did hing.
>   His blood under the altar cries
>   Foe vengeance on Christ's enemies. ''

Erected 1738.

The stone that commemorates the five luckless Covenanters captured at Bothwell Brig is located some 200 yards south of Gullan's. Nearby, at the spot where the assassination was actually committed, stands the monument known as the Archbishop's Pyramid. It is a fairly rough pile, a cairn in pyramid shape, whose stones now shelter the nests of many rats. The cairn is some nine feet high and it bears a Latin inscription telling of the deed. Entry to the field containing the pyramid can best be gained from a wicket gate into the wood off the road that runs north from Claremont Farm corner to the village of Strathkinness. The memorials have been kept in a reasonable state of repair.

The unfortunate Archbishop is demonstrated by later historians to have been a scapegoat for the oppressive tyranny exercised by the Scottish Privy Council which was dominated by the Earl of Lauderdale, himself a former Covenanter. Sharp, in fact, became a victim of the immoderate attempts made by Charles II to treat episcopacy as the established church in Scotland by allowing himself to become an instrument of the monarch's schemes. His reintroduction

21

of lay patronage was an act that touched Scottish susceptibilities on the raw and made his name detested. The nation saw hundreds of ministers ejected from their livings because they refused to comply with the new conditions, their places filled by men who were ill qualified to win the respect of the people.

By virtue of his archbishopric James Sharp was also Chancellor of the University of St. Andrews, and he was by no means the least notable in his services to the university of that long and distinguished line. He secured for it the foundation of Regius Chairs of Hebrew and Mathematics. To the latter chair was appointed James Gregory, the famous astronomer and correspondent of Isaac Newton.

The St. Andrews copy of the Solemn League and Covenant, which is preserved in the University of St. Andrews, bears the signatures of 981 men appended shortly after 1643, the year it was drawn up. These included magistrates, professors, students, citizens and parishioners. It was renewed and sworn in St. Andrews on 31st December, 1648. Many had probably been unable to sign it then, the Lord's Day, as a number of signatures were subsequently adhibited, while the Session Clerk, in the following year subscribed for 15 men who could not write themselves. There are some notable signatures including that of Samuel Rutherford, the famed divine, whose name appears three times, while the first column for students was headed by the youthful Earl of Rothes. On another page devoted to students of the same college, was the name of Donald Cargill. Ironically, Cargill was hanged for his steadfast adherence to the Covenanters' cause, and Rothes was one of his persecutors.

According to Patrick Walker's narrative, after Cargill's capture in 1681, Rothes, by then Chancellor, '' threatened him with extraordinary torture and death ''. Cargill replied—'' My Lord, forbear to threaten me ; for, die what death I will, your eyes will not see it ''.

The Chancellor, whose health had been undermined by drunkenness and debauchery, took suddenly ill and he died during the night preceding the day that Cargill was hanged at Edinburgh's Mercat Cross.

Archbishop Burnett was appointed to succeed Sharp, but he soon died. Arthur Ross became the last Episcopal Bishop of the See, but was speedily deprived of his Church privileges by the victorious William of Orange. William gave way to the insistent instigation of the Protestants and swiftly swept away the whole Episcopal structure

The ruined magnificence of the 15th Century Cathedral.

Eastwards along North Street to the Cathedral, St. Rule's Tower and the Bay.

set up by Charles II.   He annexed to the Crown most of its revenues in Scotland.

St. Andrews, thus deprived of its ecclesiastical eminence, failed to find a subsequent role in national affairs.   The city settled into a declining twilight existence as a small market town and fishing port. By 1700 it had sunk to a pitiful state of disease and decay, with grass growing in the unpaved streets.   This was only the beginning of the blackest period in the history of the once proud and ancient city. The situation was accentuated by the changing economic structure in Scotland due to industrial expansion in large centres of employment geographically better much placed than was isolated St. Andrews in the East Neuk of Fife.   Matters looked as if they could not get worse.   But they did !

At this gloomy stage, an incident insignificant enough in itself, had unexpected repercussions that boiled up to threaten the utter extinction of St. Andrews as a burgh.

In 1696 a university servant violently assaulted a citizen.   Not a shatteringly serious affair !   He was summoned before the Burgh Court, failed to appear, and was fined for contempt of court.   The University masters furiously challenged the trial procedure as an in-fringement of privileges that had been granted to them by the agree-ment of Bishop Kennedy with the Burgh 250 years earlier when he founded the College of St. Salvator in 1450.   Kennedy's manifesto, approved by James First, confirmed that " all those who belong to the university shall have the privilege of buying and selling victuals and clothing without tax or custom, provided they do not trade in these articles.   *Beadles, servants, stationers and their families shall enjoy the like privileges and immunities with the university.* . . . If any belonging to the college owe a debt to a citizen and a complaint of such debt be made under oath to the rector, he, the rector, shall send a beadle to some-one of the bailies to convene the debtor before him and oblige him to find surety to pay the debt within eight days if the same does not exceed forty shillings, but if it is more, a longer time shall be allowed. ''   For two years a bitter argument raged with in-creasing acrimony between Town and Gown on the question of jurisdiction over this minor servant of the University.

Even yet the incident had all the importance of a storm in a domestic tea cup.

c

But it was at this unfortunate time of rancour that John, Earl of Tullibardine, and later the first Duke of Atholl, was elected Chancellor of the University when he became Secretary of State. As a solution, Tullibardine revived the old proposal that the University should quit moribund St. Andrews and establish itself in Perth ! The masters, possibly in part to ingratiate themselves with the Chancellor, indicated that they were more than willing to do so. They went on to prepare a case against St. Andrews the keystone of which was a sour polemic against the city and its people. They were ' tumultuous and brutal, even bringing cannon to bear on the college gate and menacing reverend doctors with whingers ! None of the citizens loved learning.'

As to the place : ' It being now a village only, where for the most part only farmers dwell, the whole streets are filled with dunghills which are exceedingly noisome and ready to infect the air, especially in autumn when the herring guts are exposed in them, or rather in all corners of the town by themselves.'

In demanding the removal Professor John Craigie, supported by a number of colleagues, complained that :—

' The victuals are dearer here than any place else, viz, fleshes, drinks of all sorts. This place is ill-provided of all commodities and trades, which obliges us to send to Edinburgh, and provide ourselves with shoes, clothes and hatts, etc. ; and what are here are double rate. The place is ill-provided of fresh water, the most part being served with a stripe (the mill lade) where the foul fish, clothes, etc., are washed, so that it is for the maist pairt, neasty and unwholesome. The place has, moreover, a most thin and piercing air, even to an excess, which causes nitre to grow on rooms facing north where fires are lit. Old men coming to the place are instantly cut off.'

Agreement was actually reached in broad outline to transfer the University to Perth. Fortunately for St. Andrews, in a political up-heaval Tullibardine fell from power. Without further need to flatter him the masters felt less inclination for the change. Despite their indictment, couched in amazingly immoderate terms to have eman-ated from academic sources, the proposal to transfer the University to Perth fell through. Some mystery surrounds the termination of negotiations of which no record exists either in St. Andrews or in Perth.

Conditions in the city improved after this crisis but only slightly, and they still remained at a parlous level for the citizens and for the

University. This sorry twilight of a once-proud city continued for almost a century, a nadir of humiliation, hardship and communal poverty. The population sank to under 2,000.

Dr. Samuel Johnson wrote after his visit in 1773 of ' a university declining, a college alienated, and a church profaned and hastening to the ground. It is a place of mournful images and ineffectual wishes.' (P. 134).

Yet even then, in the midst of decay and of squalor, there clung to St. Andrews an ethos that captured the imagination, as it does to-day.

George Berkeley, an English student of the early 18th Century, come to the University from Eton, wrote on his arrival, of finding the town ' vexed with insolent shopkeepers and St. Leonard's College packed with rowdy and beggarly students.' Mr Berkeley wept to think of three long years in the city, if God spared him. Yet he wept harder when he came to leave St. Andrews.

Such, even in those days of her decline, was the spell cast by St. Andrews under which countless others have fallen since.

UNDREAMED REVIVAL

" If thy glories be gone, they are only, methinks
As it were by enchantment, transferred to the Links."

(Carnegie)

SEEN from the days of the early nineteenth century, the glories lay far away. As late as 1848 the population was decimated by its final epidemic of the black plague, the dreaded scourge of the Middle Ages. The city administration, falling steadily further into debt, sold off a considerable part of the lands they owned outwith the burgh boundaries. This sale included the superiority (a Scottish legal right to impose conditions in the use and sale of property) on the links of which golf was played as a local pastime. All they retained was the ancient privilege of the citizens and everyone else in St. Andrews to play their golf on the part of the links or marginal beachland known as the golfing courses.

Almost a century earlier in 1754, twenty-two " noblemen and gentlemen, being admirers of the ' anticient (sic) and healthful exercise of the golf, and, at the same time, having the interest and prosperity of the anticient city of St. Andrews at heart, being the *alma mater* of golf, formed the Society of St. Andrews Golfers ' ". Later, in 1834 they changed their name, by Royal consent, to the title of the Royal and Ancient Golf Club.

The expression written into the original minute of these fanatical enthusiasts for their little known game, that they had the interest and prosperity of St. Andrews at heart, turned out to be no empty phrase. Amid all the decay and gloom in which the city seemed in those days to be eternally enshrouded, the ' admirers of the healthful exercise ' provided the glimmer of a silver lining. Their fervour for golf steadily increased and the game began to bring a slight measure of prosperity to the city. The manufacture of featherie golf balls (crudely made spheres of a leather cover stuffed with a hatful of boiled feathers) expanded with the growing demand until it more than rivalled the only other form of industry that throve in a small way in the city. This was weaving, a manufacture conducted on 42 looms in houses in 1778. Probably most of the little old houses that were swept away when the curve of Abbey Street was recently straightened out were the homes and workshops of the hard-working weavers.

The formation of the Society of St. Andrews Golfers which became the Royal and Ancient Golf Club in 1834 was a fortunate stroke of destiny for St. Andrews. The enthusiasm of the members for their golf communicated itself to others within their own circle. They were attracted to the decaying little city, not by its history or its University, but by its golf links. Many of them first sought lodgings and later built their own houses.

St. Andrews had begun a new phase in its story as a health and golf resort. The popularity of golf was considerably enhanced by the invention in 1848 of the gutta golf ball, which, in addition to being much more durable than the ' featherie', was also very much cheaper. People, ' even of the lower classes, and artisans,' began to play.

At this time Dr. John Adamson, medical officer of health during the time of plague, had consistently warned the local authorities of the grave danger the general insanitary conditions threatened. He managed to spur them to belated action. Adamson, whose name deserves a special place in the annals of modern St. Andrews, was fortunate in enlisting the enthusiastic interest of Hugh Lyon Playfair, the city's most distinguished provost (mayor) in its modern era. Together they set about ridding St. Andrews of its squalid and unhealthy slums that had grown up around the magnificent mansions of earlier days, and of the insanitary conditions that had bred plague in the streets.

Just as earlier the University fortunes had waned with the decline of the city, so too did they begin to prosper again, although not at the same encouraging pace.

The inauguration in 1870 of the city's weekly newspaper was well-timed to catch the expansion in its population and the growth of its prosperity. This prosperity has been maintained at a steady pace from the turning point of 1848, founded on the trinity of tourism, learning and golf.

To-day, in the latest chapter of its story, St. Andrews approaches the largest population of its records. In the economic terms of the day, it is a promisingly viable proposition, with good growth potential and with its properties and assets in prime shape to be taken over. Of the new regional administration it is destined to become an important part, if only because of its international prestige in golf and its prosperous tourist traffic. It also poses for planners in the spheres of preservation and environment some highly specialised problems, including chiefly, the administration of its international heritage, the famous Old Course and the whole Links of St. Andrews.

28

YESTERDAY AND TO-DAY

" The very ideal of a little university city "
(Froude)

THE thriving golf and holiday resort of to-day with its distinctive grey sandstone buildings is very much a modern appendage to the nucleus of the original ancient city . . . . ' the city old and grey.' This modern St. Andrews dates roughly from 1830, seventy years after the founding of the Society of St. Andrews Golfers, later to become world-known as the Royal and Ancient Golf Club.

The little-known pastime of golf, goff or gowff in those days was already beginning to contribute in a small way to ease the over-strained coffers of a burgh that was poverty-stricken. St. Andrews, once-proud city, had fallen on evil times. From the heights of ecclesiastical eminence it had plunged into dire straits and dismal obscurity.

The ancient Scottish burghal system of administration emerged in the early twelfth century. It contained too many inequalities and privileges to provide a consistent revenue for the proper maintenance of the town. Changes were obviously needed and a number of drastic but communally beneficial alterations on the ancient system were made, shortly after 1800.

From then, the burghal system of local government, now in the discard, saw St. Andrews on the whole excellently served by its bur-gesses and councillors. From 1900 the town's council numbered twelve, presided over by the holder of the ancient office of provost which has existed for some 850 years. Since, in fact, Maynard, the Fleming, a merchant from Berwick, was appointed the first Provost of St. Andrews in 1124 by Bishop Robert whose ambition for himself, and for St. Andrews, was boundless. The appointment of Maynard was ' on account of his service faithfully rendered to us, King David of Scotland '. David I, that is.

The title of Dean of Guild marks the second office in age and dates back to the times when the Guild of Crafts and the Merchants' Guild of the City appointed their representatives to assume a key part in governing the municipality. Two bailies completed the magis-trates' court along with the Provost, while an honorary treasurer

29

guided the financial policy. Seven other members, also elected by the burgh voters, made up the town council.

The system had continued roughly in that form since St. Andrews was raised to the status of a royal burgh by Margaret, Queen of Malcolm the Maiden, in 1165. It had stood the test, therefore, of eight centuries. Now it gives way to a Regional system that is neither local nor central government.

In the Middle Ages, until their privileges were taken away by the Reform Act of 1832, the deans of guild continued in the full exercise of powers that were far in excess of those possessed by the later magistrates. The greatest change the system introduced was the substitution of a levy on inhabitants by property assessment to replace the mediaeval taxes of various indiscriminate kinds, such as bluidwites, window tax, salt tax and so on. It also abolished privileges of freedom from taxation on certain large property holders such as the University, the Knights of St. John and the Church itself. Until the Act of 1899, twenty-nine Commissioners administered the city.

One privilege for long exercised by the burgh itself is that of conferring the Freedom of St. Andrews on distinguished figures associated with it—a custom which the new community council must perpetuate. The honour has been conferred only rarely, seven times in all, and the last two freemen were associated with the Burgh's golfing history. They were the Duke of Windsor, former Captain of the Royal and Ancient Golf Club, and the late Robert Tyre Jones, the most outstanding golfer of the century.

Recently the accolade was extended to a corporate body, the Royal Air Force as represented by the Leuchars Air Station, one of Britain's key air defences (p. 159). The freedom was presented on the occasion of the jubilee celebrations of the Royal Air Force in 1968 and is marked by an annual ceremony at which the Royal Air Force men are entitled to bear arms in the streets of the city.

Since the dawning days of its modern prosperity, fostered by a policy of low-priced golf, the municipal resources have been wisely husbanded, a credit alike to the system and to its custodians. St. Andrews was among the first Scottish burghs to introduce gas, then electricity ; to encourage the initial building of a railway line and its subsequent extension, and to provide itself with an ample and economic water supply. Its successive municipal housing schemes, introduced by legislation after the First World War, well planned and

30

carefully financed, have proved admirably adequate to meet a constant local demand. At the present time a comprehensive sewage purification scheme, now under construction, will put the city well in the forefront of hygienic British seaside resorts ; ahead of its Regional overlord, Dundee.

James Howie, in 1871, wrote of a renascent city, " Much of the salubrity of St. Andrews is also derived from its entire want of everything known as public works. St. Andrews trusts to its colleges, its schools, its boarding establishments, its golf links and its bathing grounds. Its raw material is the human brain.''

Expressed in rather different terms, that is much the city policy to-day. No small burgh in Scotland has a more progressive record in concentrating on undertakings designed to keep it in the forefront as a modern health and holiday resort. In doing so it still managed to maintain burgh assessments that rank among the lowest in Scotland, thanks to a combination of efficiency with economy.

The city offices, which include a well-equipped Publicity and Information Centre, are contained in the dignified century-old Town Hall building that stands on the corner of South Street and Queen's Gardens. They are almost opposite the east entrance gate to the Town Church, the historic Parish Church of the Holy Trinity (p. 91). The Town Building was erected in 1858 and replaced an old Town Hall and Tolbooth, or prison, that once occupied the centre of Market Street. A recent internal modernisation, with the minimum of exterior alterations, has considerably improved the present Town Hall amenities for the public ; another major financial undertaking that was performed with acumen and economy over a number of years.

Up to within a century ago St. Andrews was a cold, treeless and windswept town, bitterly exposed on its narrow, rockbound headland to ' a ' the airts '. Yet, in ancient times it was surrounded by vast forests where wild boar roamed—the Boars' Chase, the traditional hunting ground of Scottish Kings. Even when Dr. Johnson paid his visit, accompanied by Boswell, in 1773, he saw so few trees in Scotland that when shown a magnificent maple in Queen Mary's garden, he declaimed that ' a tree might be a show in Scotland as a horse in Venice.'

Within the last hundred years a deliberate and well-planned policy of tree-planting throughout the whole city has borne a rich harvest of colour and of beauty and shelter. The present-day citizens well appreciate the foresight and vision shown in the policy of MacIntosh and, later, of Milne. These two imaginative magistrates set their fellow citizens, by enthusiastic and sagacious example, to planting trees wherever they could. St. Andrews owes them a considerable debt for a distinctively decorative arboreal feature that belongs entirely to the modern phase of its history.

In surveying their comfortable Burgh of to-day, the citizens are keenly aware that they stand at the gateway of far-reaching physical and administrative changes in the town. The former began on a large scale only some twenty years ago with extensive building development. New buildings continue to rise at an accelerating pace. How will posterity view their concrete architecture in a city of stone ?

Worthy of note is the fact that an identical stage in the process of historical repetition was reached in the mid-eighteen hundreds. Then, a building programme of comparable extent was in its early stages, mostly carried out in the durable grey ashlar from local quarries that has been couthily distinctive of St. Andrews for some generations past. It is somewhat sceptically hoped that the new architecture will age with equal distinction.

At the time referred to, around 1830, the city's wellbeing and morale were at dangerously low ebb. This was evident in the primitive public health services and educational system, as well as in worn-out domestic and public buildings. The rejuvenator of that time was ' the Major ', Provost Hugh Lyon Playfair (1842-1861.) who was subsequently knighted. He was primarily instrumental in putting ancient St. Andrews on the path to prosperity in its new role of health and golfing resort, aided as already mentioned by Dr. John Adamson, a Medical Officer who was well ahead of his time.

A parallel situation confronted St. Andrews a century later, the critical time being around 1950. The local authorities of Town and County then swung only slowly into action in the post-war years with progressive municipal housing policies and in the improvement of the other services in their charge. Circumstances combined to accelerate the action. Health and Education services, in the care of the County Council, the administrative body formed in the 1880s, were rejuvenated in the course of a massive operation which has seen in the last decade all the city schools almost completely renewed and the local cottage hospital extended and modernised as part of a new health

32

system. A clamant demand for owner-built houses followed, and continues to be quickly satisfied by the local authority, to form a steadily expanding community.

At the same time, Government policy first debilitated the University by separating Queen's College, Dundee, from it. Then it stirred the University Court to undertake an ambitious expansionist programme in St. Andrews. The results of this policy are plainly visible in numerous new buildings in the city centre and a new campus of teaching and residential buildings at the North Haugh on the north-western outskirts of the city. Students increased from a maximum of 1,300 in St. Andrews in 1965 to approximately 3,000 six years later. Their numbers still increase and the University's residential policy continues to provide new accommodation for them on the city's spreading perimeter.

From the days of the foundation of Madras College by the benefaction of Dr. Andrew Bell in 1832, St. Andrews has gained a prestigious reputation for pre-university schooling.

Dr. Bell, who went from St. Andrews as a missionary to India, evolved in Madras while he was making a fortune in India, the system of education where learning was conveyed from teacher to pupil, and down from pupil to younger pupil. He returned to his native St. Andrews a wealthy man and proved subsequently to be a bountiful benefactor to St. Andrews in the field of education.

Madras College was part-boarding school at first. Shortly after the turn of the century it became completely a day school. Since being taken over by the State as a High School it has been considerably enlarged, with a separate junior department that stands out prominently on the city's southern skyline. New primary schools have been built in different areas within recent years, replacing Victorian institutions that had long outlived their usefulness.

To-day few communities are more handsomely endowed than St. Andrews, both with public and private education amenities.

ST. LEONARDS—PIONEER SCHOOL

A public school—for girls—has occupied one of the most ancient sites in the old city since 1877. St. Leonards School for Girls stands where the original St. Leonard's College of the University was built. The school took over some of the old college buildings remaining. It is one of the best-known residential schools in Britain, a pioneer establishment with a distinguished scholastic record.

A century ago, when it would never have entered the thoughts of most women that they were in need of liberation, a group of earnest Victorians, mostly women, was preparing a daring project that was intended to liberate young women from a stultifying bondage . . . the bondage of upper and middle-class conventions which determined that if only she toiled not, nor spun, could a young girl become a lady.

This group included a dynamic and scholarly young woman who was to become Dame Louisa Lumsden, who possibly did more than any other British woman in the 19th century to bring about the emancipation of her sex. The small group decided to found a school in St. Andrews for girls that would give them full opportunity for developing their intellectual and creative gifts and to utilise them in their later lives. No such opportunity had hitherto been available to women.

The group, encouraged by university staff members, persuaded the future Dame Louisa to become the first of what was to prove a long line of distinguished headmistresses of St. Leonards School for Girls. The school was established in 1877 and moved after five years to the house and grounds of St. Leonards then offered for sale.

The founding of St. Leonards came only a few years after St. Andrews University had dealt a severe blow to the cause of women's emancipation by weakly cancelling the matriculation of Elizabeth Garrett (p. 138) after having daringly accepted her as a student.

With a delightful irony which its inaugurators would doubtless savour to the full, the buildings and grounds of the former College of St. Leonard were subsequently bought. Thus it was that the old classrooms and residential buildings where, in pre-Reformation days no woman ' save one and she must be over fifty years ' was allowed to enter, were occupied exclusively by girls and women teachers.

The success of St. Leonards School was assured from the start. Girls were enrolled from all over Britain in the knowledge that they could go on to Girton, the first college opened that offered women the chance of a university education.

How well the opportunity was seized by this daring new St. Andrews school for girls can be grasped by the fact that a

St. Leonards pupil became the first-ever girl to win a pass in Latin and Greek in the Oxford and Cambridge entrance examinations. But a greater scholastic achievement gained the accolade of a cartoon in ' Punch ' in 1887. The cartoon honoured the accomplishment of Agnata Ramsay who had gone to Girton from St. Leonards in 1884 with a scholarship. She was placed in the first division of the classical tripos, while the highest men were only in the second division.

Hitherto the subjects had been considered beyond the intellectual grasp of women. The distinction gained by the former St. Leonards girl not merely created a tremendous stir in educational circles ; it demolished the argument that certain subjects were unsuitable for girls. The incident quickly became a landmark in the emancipation of women.

Thus, as the University of St. Andrews was the first in Scotland, so has the city an honoured place in the struggle by women to gain equality in education. Indeed, St. Leonards has long preserved a close academic and administrative association with the University, one of whose professors, Lewis Cambpell, was a St. Leonards founder. In addition to maintaining a benevolent interest, the University is also the ground superior of the school and the residuary legatee.

St. Leonards for almost a century has been one of the most highly regarded and best-known schools for girls in Britain and the city has gained no little in prestige and reputation by its presence. With its group of surrounding school residences all built of solid St. Andrews stone, no school in the world has a more historical and romantic setting. The main Bruce Building on the site of the old College had been reconstructed a few years before its purchase by the School, with a Gothic front added that accorded with the ancient Chapel of St. Leonard opposite.

Queen Mary's House (p. 52) was added to the School in 1926 and in the following year, when the School jubilee was celebrated, the old mansion in which Mary, Queen of Scots, spent many happy days free from the cares of State, was opened by the Duchess of York who was to become the Queen of George VI.

Queen Mary's own chamber is furnished in the style of her time. It was there that Chastelard, her over-romantic and over-bold wooer secreted himself. Among the treasures of the house is a chair which is claimed to be the fifth oldest in Scotland.

In the western residential area of the town, New Park Preparatory School for Boys sends an annual stream of pupils from all over the country and from overseas, to the British public schools and has done so since shortly after the First World War.

In sum, reviewing St. Andrews to-day, the ancient Royal Burgh stands at a progressive and prosperous stage in its history—an ancient city with a historic past ; a modern holiday resort with a bright future ; a charming university town of unusually individual grace and atmosphere.

WATCHDOG OVER THE PAST

" There is no single spot in Scotland equally
full of historical interest."

(*Lord Cockburn*, 1842)

How to preserve buildings of the Middle Ages and yet keep pace
with the complexities and demands of the modern world is an ever-
present problem to any historic place.   These difficulties are intensi-
fied for a community that has the considerable onus of the national
heritage that is St. Andrews.

No change in local administration imposed by statute can blur,
let alone erase, its clear-cut individuality and character as a unique
Scottish burgh, no matter how complete the surrender of its administrative status.

Indeed, at this stage in the history of St. Andrews the fact was
never more superabundantly clear that in the national interest the
essential ' old town ' must be preserved as unspoiled and unchanged
as remorseless time will allow.   This is fully realised by the present
administration.   The question is how acutely it will be appreciated by
the new ?

How best can this mediaeval heritage be buttressed to withstand
the relentless assault it faces ?   The spearhead of attack is the implacable invasion of that ubiquitous weapon, boon or curse of civilisation, the powered vehicle.   Cars swarm all over the old streets, or
are parked in every corner, marring and even obscuring the city's
beauty.

Defence, we suggest, can best be maintained by segregating the
old town as an entirely pedestrian precinct.   The few physical obstacles involved are by no means insuperable.   The past that the
architecture of the old town conveys so graphically is a subject of
vital national importance and concern to the future.   It must be
preserved.

The older precincts are deeply appreciated as a responsibility
which successive generations of citizens and their town councillors in
the past 130 years have cherished and preserved with shrewd and

37

loving care. But it was only as recently as 1938 that this civic concern was channelled into concerted and constructive effort.

The Preservation Trust of St. Andrews is a fruitful Town and Gown consummation of the growing awareness by both communities of the need for constructive action to safeguard the historic character of the older town. (Town and Gown is not just a conveniently glib phrase in St. Andrews and no apology is made for its frequent subsequent use here). The Burgh's 20th Century expansion has surged on a scale undreamed by previous generations. In its train there arose soon a well-founded anxiety, by no means confined to St. Andrews itself, lest in a short time the unique ethos of the city might be, if not destroyed, irreparably damaged in the surge of concrete modernity's relentless flow.

In 1931 a joint committee of the Town Council and the University Court co-operated in action towards their common interest of enlisting public support for a policy of preservation. This had followed expressed public disquiet at the disappearance of sundry noteworthy old houses and other buildings of interest. The public reaction in St. Andrews, and indeed, throughout Scotland, was highly encouraging. The Preservation Trust was formed in 1938, designed ' to preserve the amenities and the historic character of St. Andrews by co-operation with the local authorities, by the stimulation and education of public opinion, and where necessary, by the purchase and restoration of old buildings and the acquisition of land.'

Typical recent examples have been a donation of £500 by the local authority towards the renewal of the spire of Holy Trinity Church, in order to maintain the arresting skyline of the city ; a storm of protest from Town and Gown, led by the Trust, when the Scottish Development Department attempted to thrust an unacceptable form of main-street lighting on the city. The lighting installation since secured by their efforts is much more worthy of St. Andrews. These are only two examples of many which include substantial private donations and bequests. The Trust themselves have bought a number of historic old properties and restored them with skill and taste before making conditional re-sales.

The late Sir James Irvine, Principal and Vice-Chancellor of the University of St. Andrews from 1921 until his death in 1952, was the activating spirit in the foundation of the Preservation Trust, and he enlisted generous aid from the Pilgrim Trust as well as the assistance and encouragement of the National Trust of Scotland. In the

38

To the west, the golf links and West Sands.   In the right foreground site of the new library and Fine Arts Centre.

(University photograph).

A place and a time for reflection.   Lade Braes at the Law Mill.

comparatively brief years of its existence since 1938 the St. Andrews Preservation Trust has performed magnificent service by saving and restoring many interesting old properties of the city. North Street, South Street, Louden's Close and College Street notably have benefited.

The Trust, which may well be destined to play an even more important role in the future planning of St. Andrews, is a happy example of one occasionally-controversial aspect of community life over five-and-a-half centuries . . . the sensitively ambivalent relationship of Town and Gown that was born in the founding of the university. The barometer is ever-changing, and the pendulum swung far away from cordiality, as example in 1679. That year marked a spell of bitter and tenacious enmity between the two bodies. The emotions roused then almost led to the death-knell of the city (p. 23).

Who can tell what fate would have awaited the town had the university settled in Perth, thirty miles distant as was then gravely contemplated ?

At the other extreme of the barometric scale we find, in the Preservation Trust, a particularly happy and constructive offshoot of Town and Gown co-operation *pro bono publico*. The Trust has often wisely influenced the planning authorities, both local and national.

Even earlier than the time of the Trust's foundation, Irvine again provided the spur that gained for St. Andrews, in 1930 along with Thurso, the privilege of retaining full planning powers. All other Scottish Small Burghs were compelled to surrender their planning authority, under the 1929 Local Government Act, to the larger county councils.

Within the last decade a prolonged, but on the whole, amusing ' preservation ' controversy raged when it was proposed that the old-fashioned cobblestones that were laid down in the Market Square in the days of Playfair's ' clean-up ' should be replaced by a modern road surface. The cobblestones, objected to by a few pedestrians and many motorists because of the jarring unevenness of their surface, still shake and rattle the traffic of Market Street, preserving yet something of the old world atmosphere of what was once the city centre. Cars and lorries, perforce, are slowed down to a lower gear.

For several months the century-old local newspaper, appropriately named ' The Citizen ' had its correspondence columns taken over to overflowing with letters from all over the world. The letters ranged from the sweetly reasonable to the vitriolic; from the scholarly satirical to the bluntly sarcastic.

Most savage of all modern controversies, exceeding that surrounding an attempt by the Royal and Ancient Golf Club in 1893 to purchase the town's golf links, then owned by the nearby laird of Strathtyrum, was what became known as the 'battle of the Long Riggs'.

For most of the year 1956 quarter was neither asked nor given by the embittered protagonists. Town councillors lost their seats; one even departed, embittered from St. Andrews, as the controversy raged.

Long Riggs are lengthy and narrow strips of garden ground attached to the old mansion houses standing on the south side of South Street. They are part of an essentially Scottish mediaeval pattern of planning, the houses themselves standing to face the street. Few towns in Scotland can present examples of this mediaeval planning at all, let alone in such excellent condition as the St. Andrews properties of South Street.

Battle was joined when the University Court sought to acquire some of their long rigg garden ground from the proprietors to enable them to extend their university buildings that were close by. The owners refused to sell and the University enlisted the help of St. Andrews Town Council, as the local planning authority, towards acquiring the ground by compulsory purchase. The Town Council and the population were immediately riven on the issues of Town and Gown interests and on the principle of compulsory purchase itself.

Public inquiries were ordered, and a costly array of legal talent was marshalled by both sides before the long riggs, hitherto completely unheard-of by anyone other than antiquarians, were saved for posterity.

In the light of the University's subsequent gigantic expansion on the perimeter of the city far beyond what was in 1956 their stated needs ' for the foreseeable future ', the right decision was obviously reached, even if, in the opinion of many, it was for the wrong reasons.

As with the planning of the old city streets, the St. Andrews long riggs are now well-known as the nation's finest examples of that peculiarly Scottish architectural feature. Yet their perfection has been subsequently marred by ' development ' without stirring public comment or antiquarian outcry !

As the fine example of the Preservation Trust emphasises, voluntary effort to a highly effective degree has been a notable contribution in the city's modern era by a community that has shown itself both responsible and progressive. This effort has been outstandingly successful in the attitude towards charitable and youth work. In the latter, organisations have flourished steadily under stimulating leadership. The notable example of A. N. Thom, who died in 1968 after devoting more than half a century of his adult life to the town's Boys' Brigade Company, is by no means isolated. To-day St. Andrews possesses a progressive Youth Development Committee which co-ordinates all manner of youth movements in the city and is responsible for the erection and maintenance of a modernly equipped Youth Centre that few small burghs can command. It was formally opened by Princess Anne.

Another indication of a patently responsible community is the proliferation of cultural associations within the city and university. These involve most branches of the arts and include a fine example of ingenuity and pertinacity in the Byre Theatre of St. Andrews. This unique small theatre was recently built on the site of an old cattle court, or byre in Abbey Street, once a historic thoroughfare. The converted byre had actually served an enthusiastic local Play Club company as a makeshift theatre — the smallest in Britain — for 35 years, under the experienced guidance of playright and director A. B. Paterson, himself a notable native St. Andrean. The new Byre Theatre is a memorial to him in his lifetime. Abbey Street has now been converted from a typical old Scottish Wynd into a rather splendidly modern thoroughfare fit to cope with the rush of rapidly expanding traffic. It is the gateway to the picturesque villages of the East Neuk.

With the widening of Abbey Street, the old ' Byre ' under which name it came to command a special fame in the theatrical world of Britain as a nursery for actors and directors, was demolished. Public subscription, along with a handsome Arts Council grant, assured the continuance of the Play Club and the erection of a small, but fully equipped modern theatre on the site. A regular season consisting of a catholic range of plays, even an occasional premiere, is now an established feature of the city's theatrical amenities. The new theatre itself was a handsome and welcome addition by a local architect to the general scheme of new building and reconstruction in a street that lies in the shadow of the ancient Priory Wall in the heart of the old

41

town. A very recent re-alignment of the Wall involved the careful taking down and re-building at the bend of Abbey Street of the ancient turret that was part of the twelfth century old Priory.   It has given the historic wynd a wide, modern sweep which reveals the fine proportions of surrounding buildings, notably St. Leonards School, and a larger part of the Abbey Wall that was obscured for centuries.

ARCHITECTURAL ENDOWMENT

" Ghost-like and shadowy they stand "

(Lang)

THE richness and variety of the old city's older architectural endowment leaps to-day to the discerning eye ; yet a more keenly vigilant preservation policy in past times, particularly during the last century, could have bequeathed to the present an even more generous historic inheritance.

From the ' problem ' tower of St. Rule, the ' square tower ' whose age (c. 850 ?) has never been accurately assessed, and the ruined Cathedral, begun in 1159, almost every subsequent architectural style or period, is represented in St. Andrews buildings. The ancient stoneworks on the eastern headland stand more than a thousand years removed from the newest concrete erections on the western perimeter.

In its noble proportions South Street, recognised as one of the most gracious streets in Britain, offers a rich study in domestic architecture through the ages. The twelfth century ruins of the Cathedral and Priory Pends give way to outstanding sixteenth and seventeenth century town houses, already mentioned, complete with their long riggs, of course. They include the house once occupied by Mary, Queen of Scots, in which the tragic queen spent some of the happiest days of her life.

There also stands, at the eastmost end of the street, the Roundel, distinguished by its eminently photogenic tower, the delight of generations of artists. This town house dates from around 1600. Adjoining it is Dean's Court, which is late sixteenth century, then a lovely town mansion with vaulted cellars. In the centre of its attractive paved courtyard one finds a picturesque old well and an atmosphere of academic brooding. This house occupies the site of the ancient lodging of the Archdeacon of St. Andrews. A sculptured stone bearing the arms of the Sir George Douglas who helped Mary to escape from Loch Leven Castle in 1568, is set in the wall above the entrance gateway. Dean's Court was skilfully restored by a local

43

architect in the 1950's and is a university residence for post-graduate students.

All these houses are wonderfully preserved, some possessing walled gardens that are older even than the buildings they grace. At the extreme western end of the street stands dominantly the carefully preserved West Port, dating originally from 1589, although frequently repaired and renovated since (p. 103).

Occupying conspicuously their site in the middle of the street and centre of the town are the impressive ruins of what was once a monastery of the Black Friars, founded before 1279. Background to them is the Georgian facade of the original Madras College, erected in 1834, that conceals a considerably bigger school built only a few years ago as a modern high school extension. William Burn, an eminent Edinburgh architect, designed the original Georgian structure with its distinctive Jacobean embellishments, and the two school houses, grouping the buildings round an arcaded court. Their design by the wish of the donor, Dr. Bell, complements the architecture of the Blackfriars ruin. The older trees include two century-old weeping ashes.

A town church has occupied the site of the Church of the Holy Trinity since 1412, and much of the present structure goes back to very early days (p. 91). Within its shadow is the attractive building on the corner site of South Street with Church Street. It contains the shop and offices of the century-old local newspaper, '' The Citizen ''. The original seventeenth century building on the site was gutted half a century ago for the newspaper's commercial purpose. The result was thoughtfully and lovingly restored premises that proclaim and enhance the historic character of that part of the city. The original house was the home of Alexander Wilson, ' Father of Scottish letter-founders ' and was the birthplace in 1753 of Dr. Andrew Bell, the founder of Madras College, and a munificent benefactor of the city.

The character of North Street, dominated by the University church and steeple, is deeply impressive. The mediaeval severity of the older University buildings presents an architectural challenge and problem to any contemplated surrounding development.

A much later architectural legacy stems from the city's renaissance in the building art of the early nineteenth century. It consists to a large extent of some distinguished Georgian buildings and examples of early Victorian work that derives from the Georgian influence. There stand out smugly also overlooking the new University precinct of the North Haugh a few Victorian Gothic mansions that are typical of that pretentious phase.

Provost Hugh Lyon Playfair, when he finally roused 19th century St. Andrews out of a 150-year slough of despond, directed an almost fanatic zeal to his task. He proceeded to ' ding doon ' numerous decayed erections of the previous two centuries that had failed to withstand the combined ravages of neglect and of time. He undoubtedly destroyed in his zeal picturesque buildings that preservation could have saved to the city's advantage, but in sum, he did much more good than harm.

The ' Major ' as he was best known in his own time, had returned from the Army in 1832 to St. Andrews where his father had been a distinguished academic. Between then and after his death in 1861 the new city arose, largely due to his energy and enterprise. By then it was a gas-lit town of newly paved and cobbled thoroughfares, of new streets such as Bell Street and Greyfriars Garden. Many new houses, holiday houses and permanent homes for the wealthy golfers who were being attracted to the golf links, were built, and also a number of new shops. In the main the newer central buildings formed a striking contrast to those they replaced, and to those remaining. They were larger, more spacious and of better appearance. They had a similarity of formal style that was dignified, if slightly severe, and they still stand out strikingly in their conformity, from the individual patterns of the remaining older houses.

To-day, with their ashlar stonework, these houses are largely responsible for conferring the marked quality of solid aloofness that characterises, for instance, Hope Street, Howard Place and Abbotsford Crescent, Greyfriars Garden and the still handsome block of Albert Buildings in South Street, on the west side of Holy Trinity Church. Gracious windows and pedimented doorways single out many of them externally ; inside are to be found many mantelpieces in the Adams style.

Among larger edifices, the earlier University building of the United College and also Madras College already noted, are essentially Georgian.

Pilmour Place and Golf Place at the Links form an interesting reminder of the early nineteenth century residential boom. They

45

were sited on a part of the original golf links which the Town Council of the day (1820) feued without the legal right to do so. The houses then built are Georgian in its most austere aspect, but again, their severity ' belongs ' to that area of the city. North Street also displays some fine Georgian houses and the old pantiled house, No. 32, has a 1618 fireplace lintel.

These are only some of the features to be noted that make up what constantly is tritely, but truly, referred to as ' the unique charm ' of the city. Many others are there to be discovered, as for instance, Union Street with two adjoining houses delightful in their classical dignity. They are now overpowered and rendered somewhat less significant by the University's modern Buchanan Building across the narrow street.

Altogether, a fair assessment of planning awareness up to the end of the nineteenth century would be that the ancient Royal Burgh and ecclesiastical city is a heritage that successive generations since the era of Playfair over a century ago have cherished and safeguarded if not always with judgment, certainly with loving care.

It was not always so. The city has known, as well as the pomp of kings and queens and the ceremony of princes and prelates, the despair of poverty, disease and neglect that overwhelmed it for more than 150 years after the rejection of Episcopacy by the nation.

So much for the historic part of the city. Unfortunately, with twentieth century expansion so rapid, the ancient precincts of the old town become a proportionately smaller area of the community with each new development. Not only so, but the modern architecture increasingly tends to trespass and intrude with jarring effect on those precincts.

Even in a university city that is conscious of its endowment and of its planning responsibilities, economics have come to play an increasingly important part in recent new building by the university authorities. Later developments by them built in concrete, on the edge of the old town have been criticised, while some nearer the city's perimeter are frankly meretricious.

The local Planning Committee, which has consisted, in essence, of the whole Town Council, stands accused of having been recently inconsistent, and not very successful in maintaining the high standard that the old St. Andrews demands. Yet a yardstick of that standard for modern buildings was set by the University in the early 1950s with their administrative offices in North Street. Subsequent new buildings allowed by the Planning Committee, notably the Old Course Hotel and the University flats, have admittedly fallen far short.

In their own new housing developments, both municipal and private, the local authority has been more successful. It has created municipal schemes that are as imaginative as any in Scotland, and the Abbey Court conception is a little gem. By keeping a tight rein on the design of private housing areas, on the other hand, the Committee has initiated, in the suburbs of Canongate and Bogward, a pleasing new extension of St. Andrews without encroaching too much on that attractive *rus in urbe,* the Lade Braes.

No Local authority in Scotland can own a municipal housing scheme to compare quite with that of South Court, one of the mediaeval mansions of South Street. Only St. Andrews could possess and utilise a property that stands on a site so distantly documented . . . . a site that was measured out as an ancient long rigg around 1160 ; a property once owned by Maynard, the city's first Provost. True, the title deeds of the latest building on this historic site date back only to 1646. It was then that James Sword, also a Provost of St. Andrews, built a ' tenement back with forecourt, orchard and granary.' A monument in the Cathedral Churchyard attests to his death in 1567, and that of his wife, Christian Brydie, who was made famous in death by the punning rhyme that was carved on her tombstone.

'' HERE LYETH A CHRISTIAN CHRISTIANE ''

———

Though in this tombe my bones doe rotting ly
yet Read my name for CHRIST ANE BRYDIE AM I ''

Perhaps the most famous owner of South Court was George Martine who acquired it after Sword. Town Clerk of St. Andrews, secretary to Archbishop Sharp, business man and also historian, Martine obviously led a busy life ! The badly worn heraldic panel of his arms is set above the entrance to this remarkable Town Council development of modern flats standing in its lovely setting that includes a mulberry tree several centuries old.

South Court was first bought in 1919 by the local authority when it was in danger of demolition, and was then split into makeshift flats.

47

The latest conversion of the old mansion has taken several years to complete but by general concensus has been amply worth it. The building and its surroundings provide an example of municipal planning at its best . . . . a credit both to the skilled work of renovation and to the enterprise of the local authority in securing its useful survival.

PASTORALE

" This rural retreat in the town's very midst."

(Knowles)

INSPIRED forethought around a century ago provided the quiet little city with a green belt that adorns and shelters it. Thus St. Andrews to-day is a pleasant place of ample parks, green spaces . . . . and trees. A hundred years ago, although it was almost aseptically clean it presented a bare and comfortless aspect and was notorious for its windswept streets and draughty corners.

The transformation that beautified the town and brought it shelter from the blasts was the simple provision of trees . . . . and more trees. They were planted in the gardens and in the streets. Most of all, they were planted in the Lade Braes, the rustic green belt that stretches through the town's centre from west to east.

What is unique about the Lade Braes to visitors is to find it an idyllic inland rural retreat, totally unexpected in a bracing seaside resort. As a bird sanctuary the ' braes ' attract practically every land species known to Scotland. The occasional early morning heron, king of the nearby marshland birds, may be startled from the banks of the little Kinness Burn and its darting trout. Otherwise it is exclusively land bird territory. The sea could be a hundred miles distant.

Industrious clerics of the mediaeval Priory utilised from its earliest days the waters of the burn to power their water wheels. They conducted its water by means of a ' lead ' or lade which ran for more than a mile to the higher levels of the Priory within the Abbey walls. Hence the name. The lade continued in existence until about 1860 when it was finally filled in. It was an open lade except where it crossed the top of Melbourne Brae, and was the scene of at least one fatality and several near drownings. At one time it turned water wheels at Claremont Farm, Denbrae Meal Mill and a sawmill at Rufflets, as well as at the Lawmill (the Splash Mill) and so on down to the flour mill at the Harbour.

The Lade Braes Walk to-day traces the path the borrowed water took then along the shoulder of the tiny glen into the Priory. Long

49

after the Priory's dissolution craftsmen such as blacksmiths, wheel-wrights and millers continued to use the lade's power. The last was a golf club maker whose workshop was in the historic Pends.

For centuries St. Andrews had stood unprotected on the wind-swept and treeless peninsula.   Dr. Johnson in 1773 remarked on the fact.   Around 1860 a local councillor, John MacIntosh, prosecuted a vigorous campaign to shelter and at the same time beautify St. Andrews by means of spreading maples, pines, firs and sycamores. His work was carried on even more vigorously by Bailie John Milne over a wide area of the city's streets and along the path of the old lade that skirted the top of what was an unkempt ravine.   It was their efforts that produced to-day's happy arboreal vista and the efforts of two men are deservedly commemorated on suitably in-scribed stones erected in the Braes.

Protected by those trees from the merciless brine-laden winds of north and east, flora, and fauna flourished swiftly.   Generations of citizens, students and holidaymakers, have enjoyed its sheltered tran-quillity.   They find a simple pleasure among its rural beauties in strolling the Braes, lulled by the gentle ripple of the burn, and blinking perhaps, in the dazzling shafts of dappled sunlight on their way down through a tracery of branches.   It is an ineffably soothing experience to saunter along lazily, knowing that the bright, inquisitive eyes of birds and squirrels are quietly observing as they skulk among the leaves and needles of wide-spreading planes and other trees.

A key policy of the local authority to preserve this seclusion of the public paths and spaces and the beauty of their setting has been faithfully observed.   In recent years the policy has been brought under pressure by the town's creeping encirclement of the Braes. The pressure has been resisted so far with reasonable success.   There did exist, however, a certain disquiet, concerning the suburb of middle-class houses spreading out beyond the Braes and threatening to encompass and constrict them.   Sufficient space was left, at local insistence, to ensure that sight and sound of habitation are screened from the stroller in the rural retreat that is close to the very heart of the town.

RETREAT FOR ROYALTY

" Is this the house that had for guest a Queen ?
How changed the times, how different the scene ? "

(*Price*)

ROYAL connections with St. Andrews in the days of the Church's power were close. For the most part the State maintained a jealous and watchful eye on the influence exercised by the Lords spiritual over the nation's subjects.

So it was that from the earliest days the rulers of Scotland were frequent sojourners in St. Andrews, with their courts. This continued up to the end of the Stuart dynasty and the coincidental fall of the bishops, both Catholic and Episcopal, in Scotland.

Thus, Malcolm Canmore and his Queen paid numerous visits ; Robert, The Bruce, was present at the consecration of the Cathedral by Bishop Lamberton. So it continued with successive monarchs until Charles the Second's presence in 1650, the last royal visitor to receive the silver keys of the city which were formally presented to him at the West Port. From then, a gap of almost 300 years was bridged when the Prince of Wales, later King Edward VIII, was presented with symbolic keys in 1922.

It was possibly those same silver keys, fashioned specially for the occasion, that were handed over to Mary of Guise when she arrived at St. Andrews in 1538 for her wedding in the Cathedral. All of the early James's had close connections with the city, but none left a deeper imprint on its history than James V, his bride from Lorraine and their tragic daughter, Mary, Queen of Scots. When Cardinal Beaton arranged this marriage for James to the 22-year-old widow of the Duc de Guise he also saw to it that she was accorded a magnificent welcome to St. Andrews. The wedding ceremony was not only a significant historic event ; it was notable in that it was the last great occasion that was to be witnessed in the Cathedral. The marriage was solemnised with lavish pomp. Mary of Guise landed at Crail, and Sir David Lindsay of the nearby Mount, poet and one-time St. Andrews student, staged extravagant pageants for her welcome and entertainment. In later years Lindsay became famous for his

51

denunciation of the corrupt and dissolute state of the Scottish Church in his Satire of the Three Estates.

Two male children of the marriage died before Mary was born in Linlithgow, a weakly child.   James himself died, a disillusioned and embittered man, within a week of her birth, and his death brought two immediate problems.   Who was to govern during his daughter's infancy, and whom must she marry ?

Cardinal Beaton, in his fortress palace that was the Castle of St. Andrews, stood out as the strong man of Scotland in trying to protect his country against Henry VIII's English rapacity.   His assassination had the unexpected consequence of bringing a French marriage for Mary closer, although Henry's death brought no change in the savage English attitude towards the Cardinal, their hated enemy.

Mary grew from ' the most perfect child ' into a handsome and energetic young woman with red blonde hair.   She came to St. Andrews a lovely woman of twenty, to escape from the worries of Holyrood, shooting amicably at the butts with a religious opponent, the Master of Lindsay, and relaxing in hunting and golf.   On her first visit she rode from Balmerino, by Gauldry and Kilmany.   The house where she resided was the new mansion of Hugh Scrymgeour, a wealthy merchant who built it in 1523.   Queen Mary's House, in South Street, is now the library of St. Leonards School.   There Mary relaxed, free for a time from the cares of State and the pulpit-sniping of John Knox.   She was 23 years old when she first took occupation of her retreat, but she had visited the city for several years, always in the Spring.   In pursuance of her expressed wishes for peace and quiet Mary prohibited the townspeople during those years from reviving their rude pastime of the Abbot of Unreason, a local version of the ancient English rouse of the summer king.   This still survives in various other towns in different forms, for instance, in Peebles as the Beltane Festival.   Up to Mary's time, at the Feast of Unreason, the people swarmed into churches to sing indecent parodies of hymns, '' and even were sometimes encouraged by the parish priests to do so ! ''   She returned again in February of 1562, and it was during that visit the Chastelard episode wrote another dark page on the history of St. Andrews.

Pierre de Chastelard, a French courtier, with his charm and romantic poetry, was graciously received by the young queen.   He made the fatal error of attributing his warm reception to something more humanly passionate, and died as the price of his mistake. One night a maid discovered him hiding under Mary's bed. The Queen was not informed. Two nights later Chastelard burst into the Royal chamber with its small oratory. Mary called for help. Chastelard was roughly seized and thrown into the Castle prison. At a public trial in St Andrews a week later, in 1563 he was sentenced to death and his execution took place in the Market Square, witnessed by the town Apparently there was more of politics than romantic ardour in the incident. The Italian Nuncio with the French Court reported that '' a French gentleman was found under the bed of the Queen of Scotland and although he said at first he had done so for love, yet afterwards when condemned to death confirmed he did it by the express order of Madame de Cursol who had sent him to that kingdom to give a bad name to that queen.' Madame de Cursol was a Huguenot of Catherine de Medici's Court.

A letter to the Pope from his agent at Trent reported : . . . It was discovered he had acted thus with the intention of killing her and had been induced to do so by the Huguenots. The Bishop of Salamanca, Gonzales de Mendoza, in his report stated : . . . As for the Queen of Scotland, they determined not to kill her, but to dishonour her, in order to prevent her from marrying.'

After Mary's marriage to the weak and vindictive Darnley, St. Andrews saw the tragic Queen only once more, and that fleetingly.

Her son James bestowed many marks of esteem on the city. By then the Cathedral and Priory had been bereft of their power by the Reformation and the spiritual centre had moved to St. Mary's College where stern Andrew Melville was a powerful Principal and instrument of the new Church. James detested Melville but loved St. Andrews which he visited on many occasions, notably in 1587. Ten years later he was publicly scolded in Holy Trinity Church by Melville who had already laid deep at St. Mary's the foundations of his Protestant ideology, and anti- royalist doctrine. Melville and his nephew, James Melville, famous as a scholar and for his Diary, so revealing of the life and times, also played leading roles in the General Assembly of 1596. The King called the Assembly to his palace at Falkland. He listened patiently to James Melville for whom he had regard and a considerable respect. But the short-tempered Andrew could not refrain from ranting and wound up by calling his King ' God's sillie vassal.' Not unnaturally, his career in St. Andrews ended under heavy royal displeasure.

After the Union of the Crowns there was no further visit by James until 1617 when he addressed the Scottish clergy in the Castle Chapel.

Queen Mary's House was also occupied by Charles II on his brief visit when he was welcomed at the West Port.

In recent years, King Edward VIII as Prince of Wales came to St. Andrews to play himself in as Captain of the Royal and Ancient Golf Club, an office subsequently filled by his royal brothers of York (King George VI) and Kent in 1930 and 1937 respectively. The city has since had visits from Queen Elizabeth, the Queen Mother, and from Princess Anne. Various members of the Royal Family, including Queen Elizabeth and Prince Philip, have frequently visited nearby Leuchars Air Station (p. 159).

A striking reconstruction of a noted old building in South Street.

South Court, a 16th Century mansion, now a unique municipal
housing restoration.   A mulberry tree is on the left.

HISTORIC MARKETS

'' As in a dream I saw the ancient town
Disporting on the eve of Senzie Fair.''

(*W. M. Neill*)

OF the five annual markets that were a burghal institution in mediaeval days the solitary one remaining to-day is the Lammas Fair, the
only annual market still allowed to disrupt the central streets of a
busy and thriving city by its existence. It is also the oldest surviving
mediaeval market in Scotland.

A charter to the Burghers of St. Andrews to continue their five
traditional annual fairs was granted on the petition of Archbishop
Gladstane by King James VI in 1620, and it was confirmed by an Act
of the Parliament of Charles I. This charter proceeded on the narrative of previous documents. The first one was granted by Malcolm
the ' Maydin ' as far back as 1153, thus testifying to the antiquity of
these trading markets. These fairs were held on ' holy days ' of the
calendar of saints of the Roman Church, and the first and most important of these holidays was the Senzie Fair which continued for the
space of fifteen days, beginning on the ninth day of Easter. To
St. Andrews came merchants from all over the country and from the
Low Countries. At its peak prosperity, 300 vessels tied up at the
Harbour for the Senzie Fair, and the population was 14,000. Not so
long after this, on Trinity Day, early in June, came the second fair of
the year.

The Lammas or Loaf Mass Market was originally held on the
day of Peter's Chains in Lammas, namely on August 1st, while the
fourth fair took place on the second day of Michaelmas at the end of
September. The final holy day before Christmas and the last fair of
the year was St. Andrew's Day on November 30th. To the Cloister
Garth of the Cathedral at Senzie came the traders from Europe who
provided in so many ways a broadening link with the Scottish
populace.

Sole survivor of these ancient markets, the Lammas Fair has
altered considerably in character down the centuries with changing
times and conditions, from its original purpose of a trading market.

Towards the end of the Middle Ages there came the inevitable change when the religious significance was lost, while the decline of the city following upon the Reformation also saw the trading aspect dwindle. The Lammas gathering of town and country people of the district in the eighteenth and nineteenth centuries was ideal as an opportunity for farmers to meet agricultural workers and bargain with them for terms of employment. This was its main purpose by about 1800 and at that time it was also the only place at which local householders could buy goods like copper, iron, tools and pottery. The Lammas Market remained something of a trading fair until the 1870's. By then the hiring of farm workers was the predominant business transacted. The hucksters with their amusement stalls took over from the tradesmen and barterers, and provided diversion and entertainment for the country people who were attracted to the Fair in hordes.

Even the feeing or hiring of farm servants was gradually dying out about the beginning of the First World War and the fun-fair aspect became, as it is now, the main feature of the Lammas Market. A hundred years ago the Town Band would play all day and as evening approached the Fair became a bedlam of noise, smell and drunkenness on a scale unknown to-day . . . a bucolic orgy.

Nowadays the Lammas Fair is an anachronism, recognised as such by most, but still cherished by the majority of citizens. It also carries the support of the Local Authority for two reasons ; its venerable history and tradition, and the revenue that comes to the municipal coffers from the auctioning to the showmen of stances on the streets. Regionalisation poses a future problem and question mark here. Will the Road Authorities yield to sentimental tradition and continue to permit disruption of the city's centre on the scale created by escalating modern traffic at the peak of its holiday volume ?

In recent years the increasing problems of traffic on South Street and the two-day disruption created by the Fair have led to swelling murmurings being heard against the Lammas Market. Suggestions have been mooted that it should be taken to the West Sands, or even allowed to die out. In 1961 a local firm sought in the Court of Session to interdict the Town Council on certain points concerning the running of the Fair. The contention was that the Town had no right to continue the market so as to interfere with the conduct of business in a way to cause the defenders loss ; also that without the defenders' consent, to let stances on terms which permitted showmen and their equipment to obstruct entrances to their premises, was harmful to their business.

The opinion of Lord Migdale in the Court of Session was he was satisfied that the Town Council had good title to run the Fair in the manner which it considered best. Here again, as in the case of the golf links a problem for the Regional authorities arises.

The Lammas Market, then, provides a red-letter two days on the St. Andrews calendar. It marks the climax of the holiday season and on the day following ' the market ' the town is emptied by a mass exodus of showmen and citizens, leaving visitors to wander aimlessly through a ghost town for the day. ' Carnival is over ', is the nostalgic cry. ' After the Lammas Market . . . . winter ! '

Mention must be made of one other continuing market. This is not an annual event, but the survival of the age-old weekly farm and garden produce sale at the Mercat Cross. Among the privileges granted to the city in the various charters going back to 1213 was that of erecting ' mercat ' crosses anywhere within the bounds for the purpose of setting up markets. Throughout the centuries beyond record, a produce market has been held, and it continues every Saturday, at the site of the cross in the Market Square. At one time a Fish Cross was sited at the Ladyhead, the former fishers' quarter of the city, in the shadow of the Cathedral. There the fishermen's catches were sold. It was facing the Mercat Cross that Paul Craw, the Bohemian and social revolutionary, was burned in 1433 as an early religious martyr in Scotland. He died with a brass ball thrust in his mouth by order of Bishop Wardlaw, founder of the University, ' that he might not harangue the multitude ! ' A typical example of the fanatic brutality of the times. If ghosts of the past, as some in St. Andrews firmly believe, haunt the town, a multitude of tortured spirits throngs that bloodied spot in Market Street.

The Market Place itself has long since lost nearly all of its ancient houses, but the cobbled stones are a reminder of much older days. They are also still a fruitful source of local controversy in these days of fast-moving traffic (p. 39) The traditionalists insist on them remaining while the modernists of the city writhe, frustrated, to see their removal. As to the old Mercat Cross it was replaced by one of those fountains beloved of Victorian days, and typically tasteless.

It is a memorial to George Whyte Melville, the nineteenth century novelist and poet who was killed on the hunting field.

Whyte Melville wrote verses that were made famous by Tosti's music for the ballad 'Goodbye'. The words, by one of these co-incidences that so often occur, were first published on the actual day of his funeral. Unquestionably Whyte Melville had St. Andrews Bay in mind when he wrote the words .... the bay on a stormy late Autumn day, possibly the day of the Autumn Medal of the Royal and Ancient Golf Club. He was himself a golfer as well as a huntsman.

> ' Falling leaf and fading tree ;
> Lines of white in a sullen sea ;
> Shadows running on you and me.
> The swallows are making them ready to fly
> Wheeling out on a windy sky,
> Goodbye, summer, goodbye, goodbye.'

THE MEDIAEVAL SCENE

" Though thy streets be not now, as of yore,
full of prelates,
Of abbots and monks and of hot-headed zealots."

(*R. F. Murray*)

A VIVID kaleidoscope of colour must have been the pilgrim's abiding impression of the St. Andrews scene in the days of its mediaeval glory. The colour was supplied not only by the trappings of kings, courtiers and bishops whose trammelled steeds bore them on their travels ; but by the Knights Templar and Hospitallers of St. John, the canonicals of priesthood in Cathedral and Priory, and the Dominican and Franciscan friars. All wore their own highly distinctive garb and habits.

Most romantically colourful of all, perhaps, were the crusading Knights of St. John of the twelfth century. A halo of romance and the glamour of chivalry surrounded their white mantles, blazoned with the bold red cross of St. John.

Design, not coincidence then, must surely have dictated the recent choice by the University of No. 71 South Street as the home of its Department of Mediaeval History. Here is, perhaps, the oldest property in the Burgh, dating back to the earliest days of the crusading knights. This was a part of the most important of the many possessions which the militant Knights Templar in Scotland amassed in St. Andrews and in Edinburgh. Two of these knights of chivalry were Seier di Quincy and his son, Roger, of Leuchars Castle (p. 158). Roger took his religious piety a step further than going on the customary crusade to protect the pilgrims who were then flocking from all over Europe to the holy city of Jerusalem. He built a church on his return from a crusade .... the notable Norman Church of St. Athernase, outside the gates of his castle.

The flower of Britain's chivalry became also rich and powerful. The historically-inevitable harvest of that power was tyranny and corruption that led to their final downfall in Scotland in 1309. Their properties and possessions in St. Andrews were transferred by law to

59

the Knights Hospitallers who, although of the same Order, were by no means friends of the militant branch.

No. 71 South Street was the largest and much the most important of the Templars' St. Andrews properties. It was the central house of a big tenement block, and is believed to have been a retreat for aged crusaders and an occasional lodging of their Grandmaster.

In a much later age No. 71 and 69 adjoining were combined into a palace large enough for a king . . . . or a queen. Mary, of Scots, it is told, shot at the butts in the garden.

Templars' property was not subject to the authority of the Burgh and each one was distinguished from town property by bearing the distinctive mark of the Order prominently on its structure. After the Act of 1747 which abolished the Scottish jurisdictions of the Order of St. John, the Town Council became superiors of the South Street and other properties. Despite that, the Cross of St. John still, in 1807, marked on a gable the building's original ownership.

Until 1840 the property was locally familiar as the Templars' Buildings. Known as ' encampments ' to the founders, they were later named ' preceptories ' or ' priories '. Around 1830 all Scottish Templars' property was incorporated in the Masonic Order. The St. Andrews preceptory, entitled St. Regulus No. 40, went out of existence about 1832 as such and its charter with it. A new charter was granted to the Great Priory of Scotland in a colourful ceremony in 1952 for the Preceptory of St. Andrews. The properties had long since passed into private hands. Now they are almost wholly in University possession.

The street frontage of this remarkable building gives little indication of the age of the remaining original structure. (It was extensively reconstructed in the seventeenth century and has suffered a number of subsequent alterations.) At the rear, above the inner pend entry a fine example of mediaeval corbelling gives some indication of its age and distinctive architecture. The interior architecture and stonework of No. 71 could provide no more fitting background for the study and teaching of Mediaeval History.

Forming the western boundary of this ancient Templar tenement was Baxter's Wynd, now insipidly anglicised to Baker's Lane. (This is one of the less fortunate changes inspired by Playfair. A return to the braid Scots names in the old part of the city would not be out of place). High on a gable of the tenement the visitors will be surprised, startled even, by the somewhat gruesome sculptured head that is clearly visible on the wall. The diabolical grimace of the face is accentuated by a crusader's helmet perched above the broken nose. The age of this sculpture could go back many centuries. There are some who are inclined to regard it more as the oldest local example of graffitti !

A singular beauty implicit in the scant remains of the Blackfriars Monastery in South Street commands the eye. It is believed to have been founded around 1278 although this is still a subject of academic debate. It occupies roughly the site of the Madras College grounds. The College was built to harmonise with the ruin, at the request of Dr. Bell, its founder. A black cross over their white habits was the pious badge of the Black Friars, a mendicant order that was installed and endowed by Bishop Wishart as his religious storm troopers. These grim fanatics were avowed and relentless heresy hunters, a fact that was not forgotten at the Reformation when their monastery was the first building to suffer at the hands of Norman Leslie's band and of the rabble that followed in the wake of the Reformers.

'' Befor the sunn wes doun there was never inch standing, bot bare walls,'' reported one of the chroniclers of the time.

The Provincial of the Order obviously cherished no romantic thought of becoming a martyr to his faith. He lost no time in renouncing in the publicity of the Town Church ' all the errors of popery '. The Order was disbanded and its properties sold off, the extensive ground surrounding the ruins going to private citizens.

All that remained of the buildings was the debris of the ' old palace ' which was demolished in the early eighteen hundreds and the fragmentary skeleton of the Church which stands so conspicuously in South Street and is now the last reminder of the monastery.

This church was built as late as 1525 and the mellowed ruin is its aisle or chapel. It bears the three shields of the Hepburn arms. The Ministry of Works have carried out their usual magnificent work of preservation here, including the baring of the base course. The slender Gothic window tracery conveys a touching impression of a sad, faded beauty. Inevitably the chance passer-by is impelled to stop, to gaze in fascinated speculation on days long since gone.

The drab greyish brown dress of the Franciscan (Observant) Friars, or Grey Friars, did not appear on the streets until much later, but their habit was certainly not designed or intended to convey

61

any warm impression of colour. Bishop Kennedy, founder of St. Salvator's College, also founded the monastery of the Grey Friars in 1458. This Order outdid even their zealot brethren in piety and frugal living. Generally its members walked the streets shirtless, with bare feet and scowling visage.

George Buchanan lays the blame for the razing of this monastery also on Leslie's men. All that remained was a beautifully wrought archway which, tragically for posterity, was removed a century ago. The well, which was re-discovered and cleared out in 1839, contained two inscribed stones, now in the Cathedral Museum. It hides in the corner of a garden in the street named Greyfriars, an inconspicuous reminder of the past that merits more than the scant attention accorded it.

Within much more recent years a splash of bright colour reminiscent of past days, has been provided on the streets by the warm red gown worn by the students. This, for practical purposes, supplanted a shorter gown of thin material in 1838 (p. 155). ' The old red gown ' with its Rembrandtesque effect on the St. Andrews landscape, strikes a nostalgic note for many an exile citizen and student of St. Andrews.

ARCHERY TRADITIONS AND MEDALS

HIGHLY important in the mediaeval scene was the part played by the Bow Butts, reached by way of Butts Wynd between North Street and the Scores. The Scottish monarchs demanded in defence of their realm in those warlike days a regular training in archery at the Butts by all men and older boys from twelve years upwards. James 1st in 1425 determined that ' wapinshaws ' should be held four times a year in all burghs and the nation's nobility throughout history practised there, along with the rank and file of the peasantry.

Archery at the Bow Butts was perpetuated well into the eighteenth century, particularly by the university where it was a prominent feature of student sporting life. A competition for their Silver Arrow and Archery Medals goes back to 1618. The original contest for the Silver Arrow normally took place at the Bow Butts, although the two colleges of St. Leonard and St. Salvator had their own butts for shooting. The custom of the annual competition for the best archer among the students was that each winner presented to the university a medal. The university collection of seventy medals amassed in this way is unique. The first medal of the Archery Society was won by a certain John Cunningham while others were gained by such historic personalities as Archibald, Marquis of Argyll in 1623 and James, Marquis of Montrose, in 1628. Each winner presented to the Society a medal at his own expense. Generally the medal displayed the donor's arms on one side and the figure of an archer to his design on the other. Some thirty of the collection of medals are examples of seventeenth century engraving and possess an added interest in consequence. In fact, apart from the collection of the Royal Company of Archers in Edinburgh, it is the largest surviving collection of archery medals.

For a time, it seemed, poorer members of the student body, because of the increasing size and ornateness, and consequently the cost, of individual medals, forebore to compete. This was rectified to some extent in 1708 when the size of medals was curtailed to a minimum weight of silver, allowing the poorer students to show their skill at a much smaller cost.

As long ago as 1424 James I ordered that all men ' busk them to be archers ' from the age of twelve. Because golf and football were more alluring than archery, they were to be ' utterly cryit doun and not usit.' Butts were to be set up near every parish kirk. Every man was to shoot at them six times. If he played truant, his lord, or the king's sheriff was to mulct him of a wether. But a more cunningly effective penalty had to be devised. He was to be fined at least two-pence, ' to be given to them that comes to the bow-marks, to drink.' Four times in the year there were to be ' weaponshawings,' where every man from sixteen to sixty was bound to parade and show that he was equipped with weapons of war, and could handle them.

Even as late as 1540 the statutes still recognised hand-bows and arrows as weapons of war. The competitive spirit in pulling the short as well as the longbow was always strong as Lindsay of Pitscottie (1532-92) records.

The widow of James IV who fell at Flodden, sister of Henry VIII, was a fierce partisan of her countrymen, the Englishmen in her ambass-ador's train. These Englishmen were ready to challenge the Scots to contests, but, Pitscottie says, they always lost the day. The Queen Mother at last declared herself ready to pledge six of the Englishmen to beat, at archery, any six Scotsmen, gentlemen or yeomen, whom the King should choose. James V, always a sportsman and himself an adept in the use of arms, promptly took up the wager. It was settled that a hundred crowns and a tun of wine should be the stake, the Queen to pay if the Scots won, the King to pay if the English triumphed. The field and the ground were in St. Andrews, where James Beaton, the Archbishop, was no doubt host to the visitors. The king chose three landed gentlemen, David Wemyss of Wemyss, David Arnot of Arnot, and Mr John Wedderburn, vicar of Dundee ; and three yeomen, John Thomson of Leith, Steven Taburner, and one Ballie, a piper. The names of the Englishmen have not been told. There was a keen match, but the Scotsmen carried the day and won the hundred crowns and the tun of wine from the Queen's grace and so ' maid the king werie mirrie that his men had won the game.' The competition seems to have included straight shooting at a short-distance target, and ' rovers,' or shooting in the air at a long-distance mark—perhaps the ' popinjay ' or ' papingaw,' a wooden figure, like a parrot, suspended from the top of a tall pole.

Mary, of Scots, the daughter of James, had a bodyguard of archers. She herself handled the bow in St. Andrews, at butts set up in her private garden, probably at St. Leonards. It was in 1562 that she was partnered with the Master of Lindsay (afterwards concerned in the murder of Rizzio and one of those who came to Lochleven to demand her abdication) in a match against the Earl of Moray and one of her ladies.

James Melville, the nephew of Reformer Andrew Melville, in his famous ' Diary ' records how in 1592, before the first Silver Arrow was shot for (in 1618), the students of St. Mary's College set up butts in the garden there. Mr John Caldcleuch, a Master in Theology, attempting to shoot an arrow at the mark, missed not only the target, but a number of thatched cottages beyond it, and winged in the neck an auld honest man, a maltman of the town, who had the ill-luck to be passing through the adjoining wynd. The town bell was rung, the craftsmen snatched up arms, broke open the gate of the College, and threatened to burn it down, because of this outrage, and were with difficulty pacified by Andrew Melville, with the aid of the minister of the parish, and other masters and scholars of the University.

But, in St. Andrews the butts were used, like the golf links, by all. In 1625 the Trades Guild ' took order ' with Robert Raid, wright, fining him for the gross carelessness of shooting another man at the weapon-shawing, not with bow and arrow, but with hag-but. It was really only then, when bows and arrows had outlived their military usefulness with the invention of firearms, that the nobles thought fit to perpetuate archery as an ancient pastime of skill and grace.

The competitive spirit in golf which finally superseded archery in the early eighteen-hundreds, with its structure of medals and trophies of various kinds, was nurtured by the archery societies of 1600.

Thus, an affinity between the two sports has existed in St. Andrews down the ages. After the demise of toxophily as its early nineteenth-century exponents in the town delighted to style it, its customs were adopted in golf by the Society of Golfers most of whose founder members in 1797, had been archery devotees, long practised by their ancestors of noble and royal blood.

As an arena of the ancient pursuit over a longer period than any similar place in Scotland, the Bow Butts of St. Andrews therefore hold considerable interest. They saw the transition of warlike practice give way in the early days of firearms to a period of peaceful competition that persisted for two centuries. Students of the university particularly—and their masters—indulged in the art as an absorbing pastime, with their wapinschaw for the silver arrow as the chief annual event. It was an aristocrat's sport and the students who participated were sons of noble families who came to university equipped with their bows, arrows and golf clubs. As example, when the Marquis of Montrose came as a student to St. Andrews he was equipped with brazen hagbut and a crossbow inlaid with mother-of-pearl, but he spent a good deal on ordinary bows, arrows, bowstrings, and canons and string to make ' clouts ' for target practice. He employed a boy to carry his quiver, and an ' ammer ', whose job was to act as marker. He was often at the butts shooting matches with his fellow students, the Earl of Sutherland, Balfour of Randerston, and others. There were matches between teams. John Maine, the bowyer, is mentioned (the ' professional,' no doubt) as shooting on my Lord's side, losing, and costing him six shillings Scots. The contest for the Silver Arrow was held in July and seems to have lasted two days. The last winner produced the Silver Arrow and levied entry-money from the competitors. The town drummer and piper paraded the streets to announce the start of the contest. At the end the winner was escorted by the archers, preceded by the piper and drummer, to William Geddes's tavern, where he entertained the competitors to supper. Montrose had practised archery from boyhood with his father. He won the Silver Arrow in 1628.

The archery competition among students went on, more or less continuously, down to 1754. The romantic traditions of the Jacobite risings lend an interest to the medal of Robertson of Strowan (1687), a Highland chieftain and poet, concerned in Viscount Dundee's campaign, Mar's rising in 1715, and the young Chevalier's in 1745 ; and the medal of the Marquis of Tulliebardine (1706) who was ' out ' in 1715, and unfurled Prince Charlie's standard at Glenfinnan in 1745.

After then archery suffered a relapse till 1833. When it was revived a club of around a hundred members was formed of university professors, local lairds and retired Anglo-Indian and military men. The Silver Arrow event was revived and a notable winner was Provost Hugh Lyon Playfair. With his wonted energy, he became treasurer and before long had established a clubhouse for the archers and the Society of Golfers at the Union Parlour where Hamilton Hall now overlooks the Butts and the 18th Green of the Old Course. Once he became Provost, Playfair, in the course of converting the wilderness of the Scores into a ' promenade almost unequalled in the Empire,' tidied up the Bow Butts and terraced one side of it. Then the Archery Club removed its butts to the lawn behind the United College and somehow dropped out of existence. The Union Club amalgamated with the Royal and Ancient and gave its accumulated savings towards the building of the present Clubhouse. Thus, in the end, golf decisively and finally extinguished its old rival, archery.

PRIORY'S GUARDIAN WALL

" And there it stood, each key-stoned arch rose-bound "

(*Shairp*)

AROUND a thousand yards long, twenty feet in height and built to a thickness of four feet, stands the impressive wall of the Priory to-day. Its massive strength tells, better than any words could, of the turbulent times that dictated its erection. With its fortified ramparts, strategically-placed bastion towers, and its canopied niches, the wall was built for more than providing monastic seclusion for the canons and priests of the Priory.

The Abbey Wall is another direct and tangible link with mediaeval St. Andrews. Within its vast precincts the whole town could find a measure of safety from siege. The rich and powerful Augustinian Friars built solidly to protect their full granaries and the rich treasures in their noble buildings.

Prior John Hepburn, whose arms are displayed ostentatiously in many parts of the old city, began the wall in 1525 that would eventually enclose the entire Cathedral and Priory grounds. It surrounded a vast monastic precinct which embraced 18 acres of the original township.

The Priory itself was, of course, much older and was founded by the Augustinians on the endowment of Bishop Robert in 1144. Their prosperity and accompanying swelling influence aided that ambitious prelate to achieve his aim of making his See of St. Andrews the ecclesiastical capital of Scotland. Soon the Priors had supplanted the much older Culdees whose Celtic church had stood on the clifftop long before either Cathedral or Priory were built. Their Royal preferment was all-embracing and quickly they took steps to attempt to absorb the Culdees. It required much more than a century to achieve this finally. The Culdee Church of St. Mary remained outside the walls of the Roman Church, marking the Celtic Church's virtual exclusion, but despite this religious ' take-over ' it remained a chapel-royal for a time.

67

By about 1250 the Priory had grown vastly wealthy and power-ful. But the Prior was not mitred until 1418, even although by then the Augustinians were first in rank of the religious houses of Scotland. Their Prior ranked in Parliament above abbots and all their prelates of the regular clergy. They were then at the zenith of their prosperity and owned possessions stretching across the country . . . . rich fowl for plucking when post-Reformation edicts stripped them of their wealth. Long before 1418 the Senzie Fair in the Priory grounds had become a trading centre for all of Scotland. It attracted traders from a wide area of Britain, and from Europe, encouraging an ex-panded intercourse in many directions for St. Andrews, in commerce, agriculture and in learning. Some of the Flemish traders played an eccentric game with a ball and a stick, either on ice or over moorland, known as Het Kolven. By 1457 a similar type of game was well established in St. Andrews. It evolved into a pastime that became known as golf !

Nothing is more dramatic in the St. Andrews story than the swift and total dissolution of the Priory following on the Reformation. For over three hundred years it held pride of place as the wealthiest and most powerful institution in the city. Its Prior stood next to the Bishop of the See himself in importance.

Yet, within a few years after 1559 the buildings were being described as 'sadly decayed ' although no record exists of serious damage having been done to them in the cataclysm of the Reformation. Some of the canons made hurried confession and departed ; others became ministers of the Reform Church ; a few married and continued to live in the grounds.

But the fat Priory revenues were quickly filched by the predatory nobles, and the Regent Moray secured most of them. Without main-tenance the properties quickly fell into disrepair. The Priory became a temporal lordship of the Duke of Lennox in 1592 ; it lost more of its revenues in 1640 and still more 21 years later to the episcopal arch-bishopric. Of its 1559 income of £12,500, and properties at Loch Leven, Pittenweem and Monymusk, little was left by then.

Since 1840 nothing of the old buildings has survived, apart from a lone doocot. At that time practically all the land within the pre-cinct wall had been privately secured from the Crown. Gone are the Prior's House, his chapel and all remains of the Priory. Several of the Middle Ages doocots of the Priory type where pigeons were handily reared for the larder, still exist in different parts of the town and district, notably the one recently preserved by the local Preservation Trust overlooking Hallowhill and the Bogward area.

The most beautiful part of the Priory, which appears to have had no connection with the Abbey Wall, is the ruined gatehouse known down the centuries as ' The Pends '. It dates from the fourteenth century and was the ceremonial ' front door ' to the Priory buildings. Thus it provided entrance for the vast throngs to the cloister garth where the annual Senzie Fair took place on the fortnight after Easter. To it flocked Scots, Flemings, Frenchmen and Englishmen. They bought the wool, skins, livestock and salmon of Fife and they sold linen, silks, tapestry, carpets, spices, wine, olive oil, armour and the works of the smiths in gold and silver. On the western side of the cloister stood the Senzie House, or council hall. The eastern side was bounded by the dorter, where the monks slept.

St. Andrews then was truly cosmopolitan, and the chief city in Scotland, known throughout all Europe. It is not unreasonable to claim that there, within the encircling ramparts, burgeoned the weakly flower of Scotland's early civilisation.

Unusual Angle on the R. and A. Clubhouse, Old Course and West Sands.

Abbotsford Crescent, impressive 19th Century architecture.

(*Photo by G. M. Cowie*).
Once the home of Mary of Scots, now the library of St. Leonards School for Girls.

(*Photo by W. M. Jack*).
No. 24 South Street, beautifully restored example of a 17th
Century merchant's house.

GHOSTS OF THE PAST

" St. Andrews by the northern sea,
A haunted town it is to me."

(Lang)

A NOTEWORTHY feature of the Victorian romanticism peculiar to the latter half of that century was a considerable interest and intense belief even among the better educated, in the supernatural.   In that period of the late eighteen hundreds St. Andrews acquired a reputation, part sinister, part romantic, as a ghost-ridden town.

The brooding atmosphere of silent and gloomy Pends, ill-lit narrow wynds of the town and a looming background of tall spires and ruined buildings, inspired many ghostly tales.   These were for the most part, vaguely based on some of the terrible acts that comprise much of the city's distant history.   A few of those old tales still survive nurtured in the grim atmosphere of massive grey walls and mildewed churchyard tombstones.

The sombre Haunted Tower, conspicuous among the original sixteen turrets linking the precinct wall of Priory and Cathedral, is the prime source of numerous legends that are revived from time to time. Thirteen of these towers can still be counted in the mile length of the wall.

The Haunted Tower is the largest of them.   Beside it in the old days a harbour light was placed high on the wall as a guide and a warning to approaching shipping.

For years around a century ago, it had been fairly common knowledge within the city that the turret had been anciently used as a vault. It had long been sealed up and for almost as long local antiquarians had wanted to open it up.   Few of the townspeople would pass it after dark ; those who had the courage did so with many a qualm and fearful glance.

Local sentiment was against giving permission to disturb the dead, but in 1868, early on a September morning three prominent citizens, accompanied by a mason and his apprentice, having received the needed consent, secretly opened the tower.   They found ten bodies, excellently preserved, including that of 'a lovely young woman, beautifully dressed, a scarf round her head from which fell long, black hair. On her hands were long white gloves of leather.'

The bodies were quickly examined, and according to one of the eye-witnesses, one of the white gloves vanished during the period of inspection. Who annexed the souvenir is not known. The tomb was closed up and all five swore each other to secrecy. But a secret among five is not easy to keep. Various rumours soon circulated the town about the mystery White Lady in the tower, and people became more scared than ever to pass that way down to the harbour.

Twenty years later the tower was publicly re-opened in presence of the former apprentice mason, John Grieve, who had helped in the original excavation. It revealed a scene of desecration. Some of the bodies had disappeared and the rest had been reduced to skeletons by the action of the air resulting from the opening twenty years earlier.

Substantial evidence existed that in the interval of those 20 years, young men believed to be students, learning of the secret of the tower, had raided it and taken away some of the bodies, including the embalmed Lady of the white leather gloves.

The skeleton of a delicate foot, which had found its way into a local museum was said to be that of the White Lady herself !

Many articles were written in learned journals following the 1888 opening of the vault, about the bodies in the tower. One anti-quarian even suggested that they were saints whose bodies had been preserved in the Cathedral originally and that the coffins had been hastily removed to the tower when the Cathedral had been sacked at the Reformation.

'' Who shall say '', he declaimed in print, '' what sacred relics may have been enclosed in this secret vault so rudely broken in upon and so sacriligiously handled . . . . perhaps that of the patron saint of Scotland ? ''

The grim reality subsequently substantiated by records is that the coffins were those of victims of the deadly plague that swept Scotland in 1605, the young Mistress Katherine Clephane and her husband and family of nearby Denbrae, who were all known victims of the plague.

The White Lady of the Haunted Tower is by no means the only ghost frequently claimed in the past to have been seen walking the precincts of the old town—or riding through them.   Down the years the tales have included the vision of a phantom coach whose wheels ran noiselessly over the cobblestones.   Of course, it casts no shadow, that coach !   It is variously credited to the ownership of the murdered Cardinal Beaton or to Archbishop Sharp, completing his destiny-interrupted journey from Magus Moor to his Castle.

" Have you heard how the Cardinal's coach goes by,
      at dead of night, when the tide is high ?
And the morn has hid, and the wind is shrill,
      And all the city lies dark and still ? ''

The veiled nun of St. Leonard's conceals her self-mutilated face in the Pends as she glides into old St. Leonard's Chapel, or the wayfarer may suffer in vivid imagination the horror of seeing the Monk of St. Rule leaping from the moonlit parapet of the Square Tower.

At Greyfriars a headless monk walks the purlieus of the former monastery which he entered in remorse for a deadly crime, while the spectre of the Castle was believed to be the ghost of Archbishop Hamilton lingering in the grounds of his one-time palace before he was dragged off to Stirling to be hanged, last of the ruling Catholic prelates.

Even more to-day a feeling of time-in-suspension pervades the crumbling remains of the Cathedral and the massive torn walls of the Priory as the Pends hill is climbed from the harbour.   In that haunted quarter of the ' old grey toun ' of a shadowed evening the sensitive mind responds with primal instinct to the atmosphere of agelessness. Where else should dwell the ghostly legions of St. Andrews' tortured past ?   No reason is apparent why panic should surge, but reason retreats and the mind's disorder conjures up what dread visions ?

Yet, the St. Andrean scorns the superstition of his ancestors never more bravely than the moment the narrow Pend is passed and he reaches the comforting familiarity of the main street.

FORTRESS – PALACE

" Wicked deeds, mony and fell
By the men used of that castell."

(Wynton)

No ordinary fortress was the grim Castle of St. Andrews that was first built seven hundred years ago on the Bay's outermost cliff. Its bleakly ominous Bottle Dungeon, even incongruously pierced by the gleam of to-day's banal electric bulb to outline its black depths, chills the least imaginative spirit.

The remaining walls are little more than an empty shell—the shell of a palace that was once a fortress. The original castle, much greater in extent than the visible ruins show, was built as a palace in which the bishops and archbishops of St. Andrews could rest safe. They were warlike prelates those Middle Age churchmen, and handy with a broadsword at need. Their palace was assailed on countless occasions and was several times demolished and razed, only to rise again, a fortress castle, stronger and more grim, to face even more violent assault.

The key to the Castle of St. Andrews, until the days of its final dissolution, was recognised to be also the key to the kingdom of Fife and the greater kingdom of Scotland. From the first erection of the stronghold around 1200 by Bishop Roger until the French in 1547 bombarded out of it Norman Leslie and his band, along with preacher John Knox, it was the centre of an ever-shifting power struggle for the temporal and the spiritual domination of Scotland.

Its massive walls were the symbol of Catholic power. Their final tumbling heralded the end of Catholicism and the climax of the Reformation. Within those walls in the years until then was spun an unending web of calculated intrigue, conducted in an atmosphere of naked violence, brutal murder . . . . and worse. The ramparts were assailed by jealous princes and greedy nobles ; by the rapacious English and by the scheming French. Few were the months in the four centuries of the Castle's use that it was not under siege, or being repaired from the ravages of siege.

The Castle of St. Andrews in its time sheltered many of the royal house of Scotland. James I was educated there by Bishop Wardlaw, while his son, also James, was later taught by Bishop Kennedy the political precept of ' divide and conquer ' ; to break the dissident nobles as he would a bundle of arrows, by snapping each one separately. Within the sturdy walls James III was born, and during his reign the Castle was at once royal palace and royal prison. The fourth James was a frequent visitor. A parliament was held there by Alexander III, and the young King David II lived in the Castle, whence many of his charters were dated. The ill-fated Duke of Rothesay was incarcerated before being transferred to Falkland and to a callous death by starvation. Its walls enclosed a stage on which much of Scotland's story was played.

Edward I of England, after Falkirk, sacked the town and demolished the fortress after it had been occupied by Sir William Wallace, and it remained uninhabitable until Bannockburn had been fought, when Bishop Lamberton restored it. By then it had been taken and retaken four times in 25 years. Only a few years later the English demolished it and also damaged the Cathedral so badly that repairs were not completed until 1440.

The urgently needed Castle was the more speedily reconstructed ; of the two buildings, it held prime priority. Bishop Traill needed its stout walls for his own protection. In 1385 he built up his fortress home from its foundations, added a chapel and also the fearsome Bottle Dungeon which was originally intended as a granary store against extended siege, but was more often used as a condemned cell, sometimes as a mortuary.

The royal connection with the Castle of St. Andrews was cemented by Bishop Wardlaw, founder of the University, who became the guardian in the Castle of King Robert's surviving son, James. Wardlaw crowned James at Scone in 1424, and James later supported his Bishop enthusiastically in the institution of the University of St. Andrews.

By this time the successive Bishops of St. Andrews, the most powerful in Scotland, were engaged in constant warfare in defence of the Avignon popes. A later, and far greater danger they sought to stamp out was the influence of the heretic Lollards who probed into the very foundation of Catholicism by maintaining that the popes ' could not be Christ's vicar on earth '. John Resby and Paul Craw were early martyrs who were condemned by the Bishop to the stake at St. Andrews, ' to prevent the evil from spreading.' (Lyon, the historian, has pointed out as a singular circumstance that all the St. Andrews martyrs were sacrified by Bishops who were distinguished for their wisdom and for their generosity to the University ; for example, Kennedy, Wardlaw and David Beaton.) The most cultured minds of the times, it seems, did not quail from the most brutal of politically expedient barbarities.

Patrick Graham was the first Bishop of St. Andrews to be given the title of Archbishop, and become primate of Scotland in 1424, but the outstanding Castle personalities in the struggle to stem the rise of Lutheranism were Archbishop James Beaton and his nephew who became Cardinal David Beaton. The uncle, James, ' crafty and dissimulating ' as the English ambassador described him to Henry VIII, was once a student of St. Andrews University. He worked to foster the alliance with France, and both the Beatons became sworn enemies of Henry VIII. James, one of the few to defy the English monarch with impunity, ordered the burning of Patrick Hamilton, an unusually ill-calculated step for such a scheming prelate that revealed him as being strangely out of touch with current public opinion. It turned many of the people bitterly against him and his Church. The flames that scorched Henry Forrest later fanned this hatred. Politically, his intrigues, supported by his ambitious nephew, brought Mary of Guise to Scotland as the second wife of James V. The Royal wedding followed in the Cathedral after an extravagant welcome. Two sons died early before the birth of Mary, who became Queen of Scots.

When James Beaton died in 1539, David, his nephew succeeded and soon was elevated Cardinal. He defeated all Henry VIII's overtures towards Protestanism in Scotland and snatched Mary and her infant daughter from Linlithgow from his clutches and abrogated at the same time all treaties with the English monarch.

But it was the burning at the stake in front of the Castle walls of George Wishart on March 1st, 1546, that precipitated in unforeseen manner the bloody end of Beaton himself and the final crumbling of his Church's power in Scotland. Much earlier, Wishart, a preacher of tremendous power and conviction, had been accused of heresy for his harangues in Scotland and he fled to England. He returned to denounce Catholicism again all over the country. A brave man, he preached at Dundee during a plague visitation there, and comforted

the sick. Beaton first sent a man to Dundee to assassinate him.
When this failed, he was captured at Haddington and brought to
St. Andrews. Wishart stood trial as a heretic in the Cathedral where
Beaton summoned all the bishops, and was condemned to be burned
as such. Among the many spectators who braved a storm of wind
and rain to watch, two hundred men sitting on the walls near the
Castle courtyard draw-well, were blown down. Two of them were
drowned in the well. Guns were trained on the scaffold in case of an
attempted rescue by Wishart's numerous friends and followers.

Beaton is said to have watched at a window overlooking the spot
and he saw the victim strangled in the end. Not to shorten his tortures but to keep him from exhorting with his dying breath the crowd
to his beliefs.

The local Lutheran supporters, who were steadily gaining in
number, swore vengeance. They cannily bided their time and opportunity came only two months later. They gathered at dawn at the
nearby Abbey cemetery, with Norman and John Leslie, of Rothes,
kinsmen of the Earl of Rothes at their head. Norman Leslie had the
added incentive of a personal grievance, and of bitter envy of the
Cardinal. In small bands they assembled in the Castle courtyard,
' awaiting His Eminence ', and when the porter became suspicious at
the gathering they ' broke his head, took his keys and threw him in
the moat.'

Historians have speculated on the ease with which 50 soldiers
and 150 workmen were outwitted by a band of 15 men. It was one of
the most audacious coups in Scottish history and it was totally
successful.

The invaders quickly over-ran the Castle. The cardinal, surprised with his mistress, barricaded himself in his bedroom, but opened
it when they began to burn it down. John Leslie struck the first blow.
James Melville finished it, running Beaton through three times
with his sword. The corpse was slung over the wallhead for all to
see in such a way that it hung like a grotesque St. Andrews cross.
The body was afterwards placed in the sea-tower, embedded in salt,
when the affrighted citizens had gazed their fill, and been at last con-
vinced that their omnipotent overlord was dead.

The final disposal of the Cardinal's body is another of the mysteries of St. Andrews that historians find so intriguing. It is one that
will never be satisfactorily explained. The body of the most powerful Scotsman of his days was wrapped in a cope of lead, and ' to keep

him from stinking ' was covered with salt in the Sea Tower. There, according to Sir James Balfour, it was found some months later, and secretly buried in the confines of the Blackfriars Monastery. Another theory was that it was secreted away by stealth from St. Andrews and interred in Kilrenny Churchyard, 15 miles away, where Beaton owned an estate (p. 169).

But where the hated Cardinal lies none for certain knows ; still another mystery of St. Andrews. Why the body was not thrown over the Castle wall by Leslie's men who occupied his castle for months, is another of those inexplicable incidents that recur in local history. An interesting light is thrown on John Knox and his connection with the affair, in Lord Herriss's ' Historical Memoirs of Mary (1656)', which states :—

'' Now that the actors of this wickedness (the overthrow of the Castle and assassination of the Cardinal) being declared rebels, they resolve to maintain the Castle. Out of it, as is said, they had thrust all that belonged to the Cardinal ; only they detain Lord John Hamilton, the Governor's son who by accident was there that night, and kept him prisoner. In end the Governor raises a competent force and besieges the house, and batters the walls with cannon ; but at the end of three months (all this time being winter) he was forced to dissolve his men and return to Edinburgh to keep a parliament in February, 1547. The history says that these within the castle, being now free from the siege, breaks out and in a hostile way overruns the whole country, drives in cattle and brings in corns, and with fire and sword kills and destroys those whom they deem their unfriends. They ravish women, give themselves over to whoredom, drinking and all sorts of licentiousness.

'' Having settled themselves in garrison they take in John Rouch, a reformed preacher, and admits him to be minister of the garrison. He gladly accepts the charge and for their further instruction he brings in John Knox, whom he knew to be a of violent spirit. This man likewise embraces this society willingly and within a little time he so moulded the affections of the garrison, that they rejected Rouch and gave him both a call and admission, by shaking hands ; and by this admission he practised the function of ministry all his lifetime.''

DISSOLUTION OF A CASTLE

" In chains the captive labourer at the oar "

(H. D. Rawnsley)

THE Leslies barricaded themselves in the Castle and withstood half-hearted siege for over a year, succoured by supplies sent from England by sea. Then, an expert French army dispatched in 21 galleys in 1548, commanded by Strozzi, quickly winkled them out with cannon mounted on the Cathedral and on what was then the flat roof of St. Salvator's tower. What was left of the battered Castle ruins were demolished later by the Governor after the French sailors had despoiled it. The garrison, with John Knox among them, was taken to France and Knox was condemned to the galleys. Knox stoically accepted his experience as a galley slave and was philosophical enough to write a theological treatise while still a captive.

The Church was in complete power and the Reformers vanquished . . . . but for how long ?

The dissolution of Catholic dominance which began from within, began in Scotland with the callous and unnecessary act of consigning Walter Myln, the 82-year-old priest of Lunan in Angus to the flames of a martyr's pyre at St. Andrews in 1558. This murder of an aged, infirm man aroused feelings of utter repugnance throughout all Scotland. No one could be found in St. Andrews who was willing to carry out so outrageously inhuman a deed. The citizens refused to sell or lend a rope to tie the aged man to the stake. Myln died on the heights of the cliff midway between Castle and Priory. The execution was almost certainly a measure of the growing panic in the Church (p. 85) as the tide of Reformation surged.

John Knox was released from his galley slave captivity a year afterwards, in fateful 1559. He hurried at once to St. Andrews and found there the backing to give him support to defy Archbishop Hamilton who had ordered the murder of Myln. Knox preached in the town, and he preached more openly than ever before against Catholicism. According to McCrie " Such was the influence of Knox's doctrine that the provost, bailies and inhabitants of St. Andrews harmoniously agreed to set up the reformed worship in the town ; the church was stripped of its images and pictures and the monasteries pulled down.'' The tide of anti-Roman feeling, disgusted by the corruption, cruelty and lewdness that for long had been openly practised within the Church, was now in full flow. Within weeks the Reformation was an accomplished fact of devastating completeness. In June of that year Hamilton had ruled over a fully-furnished Cathedral, equipped with some forty chaplains of private altarages ; an Augustinian Priory of prior, sub-prior and 34 canons ; a provost and 12 prebendaries of the Church of St. Mary on the Kirkheugh ; a Dominican and a Franciscan monastery ; also a teaching clergy in three colleges. A month later all was gone. The Archbishop himself died on the gallows at Stirling in 1571.

The structure of the Catholic Church in Scotland was totally demolished and the Reformers were now the spiritual commanders of St. Andrews and of Scotland. The Rev. Charles Goodman, who was a friend of Knox in Geneva, became briefly their titular head in St. Andrews, where the staff of St. Mary's almost entirely went over to the new faith. The professors of St. Salvator's remained Catholic, and resigned. The upheaval was immense. Revenue, lands and property were confiscated, and the buildings were looted and in some cases destroyed. The University ceased to be Catholic.

Just as the churches were stripped of their symbolic fripperies, the Castle, much more the symbol of Catholic power and dominance, was allowed to fall into ruins.

The young James VI freed himself in 1583 from bondage after the Ruthven raid by taking shelter in the castle which was described then as newly fortified. But no real attempt was made to restore it.

Possibly the last official use made of the Castle was when James VI addressed the Scottish clergy in its chapel in 1617. James had built his hopes then of establishing through Archbishop Gladstanes an episcopal system in Scotland. Parliament ordered its repair by the city in 1645 but nine years later the city council had the slates and timbers removed from the Castle fabric and sold to defray the cost of repairing the pier after a storm. Down the years, as with the Cathedral, a vast amount of the fabric was spirited away to form stonework in other buildings in the city.

Archbishop Spottiswoode complained in 1629 that the Castle was ruinous. Finally, around 1635 he removed his residence to the New Inns in the Priory precinct. The gateway to the New Inns in the Pends, is still well worth an inspection despite having been twice damaged and rebuilt. By order of Parliament the Town was commanded to repair the Castle. This was in 1645 and in the following year the Archbishop's son, Sir Robert Spottiswoode and five other men of noble family, including James, Lord Ogilvie, afterwards the Earl of Airlie, were confined there, although not in the Bottle Dungeon.

Ogilvie made a romantic escape from his prison by exchanging clothes with his sister when she was allowed to visit him on the eve of his execution. His companions were beheaded at the Mercat Cross, and although Parliament offered a reward of £1,000 sterling for Ogilvie's recapture, dead or alive, he managed to ride out the political storm until later days.

From then, the Castle decayed into a weed-infested ruin, crumbling with the years, and denuded of its fabric in much the same way as the Cathedral. The slates and timbers were sold in 1656 to help defray the expense of repairing the Long Pier. Later a hundred cart loads of stonework were transferred to repair St. Salvator's.

The only intact remains of the Castle to-day are the Bottle Dungeon and the subterranean tunnels, known to every school child in Scotland. The Dungeon, even although lit by electricity, reeks still in its forbidding gloom, of its morbid uses when it was not a granary, and repels most visitors as a ghoulish relic of dark days. The inside diameter at the top is less than five feet. About a quarter way down it widens out to fifteen feet in breadth, and it is twenty-four feet deep.

The subterranean tunnels were discovered in 1879, carved out of the solid rock below the foundations. Workmen demolishing the old cottage that was a perquisite of the Keeper of the Castle, uncovered it. The main passage which can be easily negotiated, meets another diverging passage at a point where it suddenly narrows. Further progress can only be made by descending through a hole in the floor. This hole gives easy access to a large chamber underneath. The two tunnels are unusual Middle Age examples of engineering feats of mining and counter-mining. They are interesting reminders of the long siege of the Castle following Cardinal Beaton's death. The well in the courtyard which was for long covered up in debris, was uncovered in 1857. It sinks to a depth of fifty-one feet.

GRIM MONUMENT OF MARTYRS

" Capital city of darkness "

(Simson)

THE names of four of the martyrs who died at the stake in various parts of the Burgh during that frantic sixteenth century period prior to the Reformation are commemorated on an unpretentious monument that was designed by a Government architect in 1832. Overlooking the ancient Bow Butts where archery wapinschaws were customarily held, and also the Royal and Ancient Clubhouse, the edifice stands somewhat uneasily out of place in its surroundings.

The men who died as heretics, by the manner of their end as much as by the reasons for their horrible deaths, did much to bring about the Reformation and the horrors in its wake. This was particularly so in the case of the last of them, Walter Myln, the decrepit old priest of Lunan, near Montrose. ' Having ceased to perform mass, he was immediately brought to St. Andrews and found guilty of heresy, and condemned.'

We quote Grierson : "the fate of this infirm old man who, being upwards of eighty years of age, was unable to walk without aid to the place of execution, produced in the minds of the populace who witnessed it, the utmost horror and indignation. So strongly were these sentiments expressed that it put an end to such scenes for the future." This was, in fact, the final execution by the Catholics in Scotland, for heresy.

Patrick Hamilton was burned in front of St. Salvator's College in 1528 ; Henry Forrest, on the north side of the Cathedral in 1533 and George Wishart, in front of the Castle in 1558. Earlier, Paul Craw, a Bohemian, died near the Mercat Cross in 1433, but his name is not recorded on the monument.

The young Patrick Hamilton was a graduate of St. Andrews University of noble family. After spurning offers of leniency, if not pardon, for his daringly expressed views, he was suddenly seized and three days later died at the stake in agony when his burning was prolonged by the shocking incompetency of his executioners. Referring

85

to the sickening event, a writer of the nineteenth century described the city where such scenes could take place, as " The Capital of the Kingdom of Darkness." Forrest, also named on the monument, died for proclaiming Hamilton as a martyr. Two others, Gourlay and Straiton, suffered at one stake together, for denying the supremacy of the Pope. This was in August, 1534. George Buchanan, Principal of St. Leonard's College and famous for his satirical writings, was also seized by the church authorities and imprisoned in the Castle of St. Andrews. Buchanan was fortunate. He managed to escape and make good his retreat to the safety of England. He returned later to become a leader of the Reformed Church.

The execution of George Wishart, agent provocateur of the Reformation and an eminent preacher of its doctrines, took place in the midst of a hurricane at the foot of Castle Wynd, and directly opposite the castle window of Cardinal Beaton. Historians give conflicting accounts of his end. According to Archbishop Spottiswoode the last words by the martyr as the flames devoured him were : " This flame has scorched my body, yet hath it not daunted my spirit ; but he who from yonder high place beholdeth us with such pride, shall in a few days lie in the same as ignominiously as now he is seen proudly to rest himself." That his executioner would ever have allowed these romantically brave words to be delivered is hopelessly improbable. The rope around the victim's neck would have been tightened to prevent him from speaking, even had he been physically able to do so.

But, fifteen months later Cardinal David Beaton himself was assassinated in the daring sortie on his castle by Leslie's bold party of Fife conspirators . . . . the coup which later led to the later demolition of the castle (p. 78).

The places in the streets where some of the martyrs met their deaths are marked with crosses within circles. Thus one will be found in Market Street at the site of the Market Cross. There is also one in North Street at the gateway to the University where Hamilton was burned, and another at the foot of North Castle Street opposite the Castle where Wishart was martyred.

In the heart of St. Leonards School for Girls.

The 16th Century West Port under which now flows an endless
stream of 20th Century traffic.

The new sport of sand-racing at the West Sands—Britain's finest
site for the sport.

THE SHAME OF A CITY

" Scriptures plainly counsel give ;
' Suffer not a witch to live ' ".

(C. B. Gunn)

ONE of the loveliest vistas of St. Andrews is the sweep of the Bay and coastline from the clifftop that overlooks the Step Rock Swimming Pool. Difficult, therefore, to realise that this place marks the most shameful period in the story of St. Andrews ; the scene of some of the blackest deeds in the Burgh's history, and, indeed in the history of Scotland.

For this is the Witch Hill from which unfortunate women and men were cast into the Witch Lake below to undergo the grisly, ironic test of flotation. If the victims swam, then it was to the stake, for they were truly witches, If they did not, they drowned, or were rescued from drowning for a worse fate.

A fierce, but admirable faith in their religion inspired the earlier Scottish martyrs such as Wishart and Hamilton and the rest to die terribly for its sake. But no such spirit engendered the even fiercer, fanatic zeal of the Reformers that continued to burn searingly in Scotland far beyond the first frenetic days of their triumph.

For it was the bigotry within the new church order to seek out and scotch ' ungodliness ' that led to this revolting epoch in Europe that was prosecuted in no other country as vigorously as in Scotland ; in Scotland nowhere as furiously as in the St. Andrews area—the era of the witch hunts.

Immediately following the Reformation most of the Catholic clergy throughout the country resigned themselves to the new order and some of them became Protestant ministers. For a time the presbyters of the kirk sessions became all-powerful and dominated their ministers. The hot-headed bigots among them, inflamed by the Old Testament text, became responsible for promoting what amounted to trials of inquisition. Those zealots—and Holy Trinity Church of St. Andrews, appeared to have a full share—gloried in their power and self-righteousness. Inflamed by the outpourings of Knox, the

G

87

hunt was prosecuted with a fanatical fury in St. Andrews, more intense because this was the city that was so recently the Catholic capital.

Without question the mob's superstition was often whetted to provide a weapon of political intrigue for their overlords. For example, William Stewart, a former Lord Lyon King of Arms was hanged in 1569 for the crime of necromancy. His accuser was his arch-enemy, the Earl of Moray ! Ironically, the use of evil powers was alleged against Knox himself. He was accused of having used witchcraft to secure the consent of marriage to his second wife, Margaret Stewart, daughter of Lord Ochiltree. It was also alleged that by the black art he drove his servant, John Ballantine, to madness and to death !

The wild allegations failed, but there can be no doubt that political use was extensively and cold-bloodedly made of accusations of witchcraft.

For a number of years the religious fanatics of St. Andrews ran riot, and the passage of time did little to calm their burning fury. From 1569, when they burned their first witch at the stake, until 1705, when Janet Young, a crone living at the west end of Market Street, was put to death as the last witch of St. Andrews, there passed 150 years of terror. This was a date later than the burning of the last witch of Salem in America, and the inhuman Scottish witch statutes were not repealed until as late as 1735. The hunt was prosecuted with a hellish zeal. Kirk Session minutes show how church elders elected themselves judges and juries of their neighbours' morals and conduct. The repentance stool that is still an exhibit in Holy Trinity Church was often in use to humiliate and purge the ' ungodly ', while the elders looked on in unctuous satisfaction. It was the least of the punishments.

Much fiercer burned the zeal to seek out witches. Neither high nor low was spared in the gloating eagerness for blood. John Knox showed no Christian charity nor mercy in 1572 when a ' witch ' was set up on a pillar before him to suffer the scalding blast of his tongue before scorching flame was set to the faggots round her feet. Mother MacNiven was another such.

How many perished at the Witch Lake by drowning is a matter for conjecture, but a long succession of ignorant, terrified old women died agonisingly there. A great quantity of bones was cast up on the

88

little beach of the Witch Lake by an unusually severe storm in 1856, grisly relics of a shameful period in Scottish history. The lower fragment of a wooden tie-post, enclosed by masonry, thought to be a witches' stake, was also washed up. St. Andrews and its surrounding area of the East Neuk of Fife was satanically assiduous and forty witches met their death in this area in 1643 alone.

Slightly on the credit side of the St. Andrews Kirk Session was the case of Margaret Aitken, the notorious beldame of Balwearie. A confessed witch, she, to save herself, turned smeller-out of other witches. Aitken was carried around Fife on her dread mission for which she claimed that as a witch she had a special gift. Witches "had a secret mark all of that sort in their eyes, whereby she could surely tell, how soon she looked upon any, whether they were witches or not."

St. Andrews Kirk Session urgently petitioned the King to repress the abuse of carrying witches about for this purpose.

Even in those credulous days Aitken's accusations came to be received with suspicion and when she eventually met the fate she had consigned to many others, she repudiated every one of them.

Pittenweem, within the ecclesiastical orbit of St. Andrews, gained an unenviable notoriety for witch-hunting. "Several persons were tried, condemned and executed", states Connolly in his ' Memorials of Fife '. "This was done with a refinement of cruelty in that the nearest relatives were made to pay the expenses of execution."

A ghoulish ritual accompanied the trial of witches. Before being cast into the water the right thumb of the suspected person, generally a woman, was sometimes tied to the great toe of the left foot—otherwise the proof was not deemed to be canonical, as the accused was not crossed ! Sinking did not involve drowning, because a rope was attached to the victim's waist. Death in some crueller form invariably followed.

The only slight mitigation to be put forward for the accusers, was, as Kirkpatrick Sharpe wrote : "It ought not to be forgotten that many of these persons made a boast of their supposed art in order to intimidate and extort from their neighbours whatever they desired; that they were frequently of an abandoned life, addicted to horrible oaths and imprecations ; and in several cases vendors of downright poison, by which they gratified their customers in their darkest purposes of avarice or revenge."

89

Around the beginning of the eighteenth century there came a final recrudescence of the mania. In June, 1704, at the time when Janet Young was the last woman to be burned in St. Andrews, five women and two men were imprisoned by the bailes of Pittenweem. One of the women, Janet Cornfoot met a shocking end at the hands of a rabble of local fishermen, after three hours of torture. She had managed to flee to Leuchars, but the minister there pitilessly sent her back to her doom under the charge of two men. They arrived in winter and late at night. The mob met her and dragged her to the shore. Three times she underwent the flotation test for witchcraft before she was dragged ashore, and pressed to death by a weight of stones on a loose door being piled on top of her.

In a dark corner near the gate house, and significantly outside the burying ground of the recently restored Priory of Pittenweem is an unhallowed spot. It is said to be the last resting place of a number of the ' witches ' of Pittenweem. They were denied, as witches, burial within the consecrated ground of the Priory.

THE TOWNSPEOPLE'S CHURCHES

MYSTERIES OF HOLY TRINITY

" Where Mary wept and iron Knox could pray "

(W. L. Courtney)

MYSTERIES hold a special fascination for most people. No fewer than three intriguing puzzles attach to this Church of the Holy Trinity, the Parish Church of St. Andrews, a noble building which has occupied its central site in South Street, the city's spacious main street, for upwards of five-and-a-half centuries. Holy Trinity is a direct link with the earliest days of Scotland's history, although its fabric has undergone many renovations.

The dominant seventy-four foot tower and parts of the west front of the church are all that are left of the original structure, but the grand scale of its mediaeval architecture as conceived in 1412 is faithfully reproduced in the successful and wholly admirable renovation of 1909, the latest and finest of a number of restorations of the fabric through the centuries.

Nor was the 1412 edifice the first Holy Trinity. The original Town Church was situated somewhere near the east gable of the Cathedral. It is mentioned in a Papal confirmation of 1163 as the Church of the Holy Trinity of Kilrimund and was rededicated by Bernham, one of the early bishops, in 1243.

To give some idea of its size and importance, thirty chaplains principal and twelve choristers regularly officiated in honour of St. Andrew in 1475 and there were at least twelve altars in the church.

How long Holy Trinity has been known as the Town Church is a matter of conjecture. The practice is believed to have originated to indicate a church that was used by the townspeople as distinct from the ecclesiastics who thronged the Cathedral. It would appear therefore to be not so much a post-Reformation term, but a time-honoured usage infinitely older.

The earliest mystery attached to Holy Trinity concerns the origin of what is possibly the oldest authenticated Christian relic in ancient St. Andrews. This is a stone in the tower that forms part of

91

the passage roof leading to the top of the side aisle wall. It is clearly a tombstone, and a rudely incised cross and other emblems are visible on it. From its character and the use to which it has been put, the tombstone is considerably older than 1412. Antiquarians have no clue to its source, although some contend it must have come from the original church of the Holy Trinity that was erected by Turgot beside the Cathedral for the use of the townspeople in the first Town Church.

The lovely Holy Trinity of to-day contains many relics of the past and is one vast museum of the city's history. The tower was not in the early days just used as an ornamental lookout post. In the sixteenth century it was a forbidding prison or house of correction for errant women. There were many allegedly such who were driven by fanatic Reforming zeal up the steep stair to the dreary prison above to reflect for a time on the error of their ways.

The main entrance to the church is by way of the great porch that was built in memory of John Knox, that most zealous and unbending of the Reformers. It was in the Town Church that Knox preached his famous first sermon in which he denounced and undertook to prove the degeneracy of the Roman Church. Whatever else, Knox was a courageous man of his faith, for he risked a fearful death by doing so.

From his contemporary, James Melville, we get a graphic description of the almost fanatic fervour of Knox, when sick near to death, he preached his final sermon in Holy Trinity. '' Richard Ballanden (Ballantine), his servant, and another, lifted him up to the pulpit whar he behovit to lean at his first entrie ; but, or he had done with his sermont he was as active and vigorous that he was like to ding that pulpit in blads, and fly out of it.'' So wrote Melville.

Is the pulpit that Knox's fervour was apt to '' ding in blads '' the same that now has an honoured place in the University Chapel ?

This is highly unlikely. That pulpit was discarded by the Town Church in the extensive renovation of 1798 when even the gallery, locally known as ' the sailors' loft ' was sold to the Burghers' Church. It is believed to be dated around 1580, or post-Reformation. If it had been that which from Knox preached, the Session would scarcely have let it go, even to the University. In the extensive fabric reconstruction many people were allowed to carry away carved woodwork to save it from destruction. The pulpit was sold to the University.

Only two oak stalls survive to-day in the church as original wood-work of mediaeval days. It is believed Mary, Queen of Scots, sat in one, according to unverified tradition, and the Royal Arms are certainly carved on the side of it. The other bears the Bishop's arms.

The renovation of 1800 saw the church fabric considerably altered, with higher arches built at the expense of taking away every second one of the original pillars of 1412. The external walls were heightened to make space for a deep gallery for about 900 people, which was carried right round the building. This renovation continued in use until June 2nd, 1907, when the last service was held before the successful latest restoration which was completed in 1909. Indications of the various alterations of 1642, 1767 and 1800 are readily traced in the fabric by the observant.

The artistry of Dr. P. McGregor Chalmers, the architect, gave back to the city in 1909 the authentic form of its ancient church. Leading promoter of the restoration, dreamed of for many years, was the Rev. Dr. Patrick Playfair, minister of the first of the two charges that comprise the church. R. G. Cant, the University historian, points out that in order to recapture the original design of the church it was necessary to undo almost all of the reconstruction of 109 years earlier. For many of the details the architect made use of his vast knowledge of Scottish churches and other buildings of the Middle Ages.

The hub of church life in early St. Andrews was the Cathedral until June 1559 by which time it had become unfit due to dilapidation, for purposes of worship. From then on the Town Church became the centre. It witnessed many strange scenes both before and after its elevation brought about by the Reformation. The Church possesses the oldest Kirk Session minute in existence dated 1559, the year of Reformation. The Session met weekly and the elders could be fined for absence or arriving late or leaving early. The ministers of those troubled days took themselves as God's representatives and their duties solemnly and with a grim seriousness, only outmatched by their Session. A few years after Knox, Robert Wallace, a minister of Holy Trinity, was preaching in the church to the King and was interrupted by His Majesty. '' Whereupon Mr. Andro (Andrew Melville, Principal of St. Mary's College, and the founder of Presbyterianism in Scotland) rebuked the King verie sharplie and threatened him with the judgement of God if he repented not.'' Some years later Melville was to go much further in criticism of his king (p. 133).

93

Royal visits to Holy Trinity in those days were not infrequent and there is record of King James VI and 1st, in 1617, listening to a Latin oration made in name of the University by the Rector, Mr Peter Bruce, the Principal of St. Leonard's College.

John Douglas, first of the Tulcan archbishops, died in the church pulpit. Tulcan episcopacy itself died with Archbishop Adamson.

Of compelling interest to every visitor is the overpoweringly impressive marble memorial to Archbishop James Sharp, the victim of the Magus Muir assassination (p. 19). To accommodate it the east wall of the south aisle was considerably raised in height towards the end of the seventeenth century. Sharp, who had been a Presbyterian minister in nearby Crail, came to St. Andrews in 1662, following a visit to London, elevated as the Episcopal Archbishop of St. Andrews by appointment of King Charles II and supported by a vast retinue of horsemen. His first sermon was delivered in the Town Church on the Sunday after his arrival. It consisted of a vindication of himself and a vehement advocacy of Episcopacy. Thirteen days after his murder in 1679 at nearby Magus the corpse of the Archbishop was borne with great pomp and circumstance to the Town Church for burial. Draping the coffin was the bloody gown he was wearing when he was killed.

Sharp's tomb is marked by the massive monument in marble, of Dutch origin, that was erected by the Archbishop's son who mortified a sum of money for its upkeep. It is well preserved despite there being a record that in the seventeenth century the church was broken into and the monument defaced. When the tomb was opened in 1849 the vault revealed only some coffin handles and broken wood. Of the prelate's bones there was no trace !

How could such a major undertaking as the opening and despoilation of the tomb have been carried out without the knowledge of the Kirk Session ? Was it that some perfervid Presbyterians could not thole the thought of an apostate's bones lying in state in their church ? The stealthy deed must rank as the best-kept secret of St. Andrews.

Sharp's monument bears a long inscription in Latin, telling the narrative that ' a band of nine parricides, through the fury of fanaticism, and in the vicinity of his metropolitan city in the light of noonday, cruelly murdered him with many wounds from pistols, swords

94

and daggers, while his eldest daughter and domestics, while wounded and weeping, sought to protect him.'

Holy Trinity contains other memorials of Sharp who, notwithstanding the hatred that surrounded him, proved a considerable benefactor of the Town and the University during his rule. His gifts include a baptismal basin and laver, engraved with his arms, which are perhaps the most historic of numerous ornaments donated to Holy Trinity down the centuries. These include valuable sacramental plate and six communion cups.

Several other bishops are buried in the Town Church.

Not at all beautiful are other relics still contained within Holy Trinity . . . . instruments of the Church used in more rigorous times than to-day to induce a proper spirit of Christian humility in recalcitrant members of the congregation. These possess a repellant fascination. The most innocuous of them was the penitent stool in constant use in the early days of the Reformation and the dying days of episcopacy. Never was it easy to produce the proper penitential spirit in sturdy Fife individualists. More than once the all-powerful Kirk Session had to decree that ' na persoun sall cum to the stuil armed with sword or gun '.

The cutty stools, as the stools of repentance were known, were used in the disciplining of the parishioners, and are of considerable age. A sackcloth shirt is of interest, but not so repellant as the fearsome ' branks ', an instrument used to still the tongue in brutal manner, of those convicted of scandalous and blasphemous language. Tradition relates that Archbishop Sharp in 1673 caused these particular branks to be used to silence a woman, Isobel Lindsay, who several times had the temerity to speak up against his preaching. Isobel had previously been dealt with by the Presbytery for railing at the Archbishop, obviously without avail.

The ornamentation throughout Holy Trinity Church, the carvings and the stained glass windows are notable. They are described in detail in the Historical and Descriptive Notes of the Church. Six beautiful communion cups of varying age are part of the church plate. A mural tablet to Old Tom Morris, the first professional of the Royal and Ancient Golf Club, and a lifelong pillar of Holy Trinity attracts the interest of golfers from all over the world.

Above the ornate Boyd Memorial lectern limply hangs a battalion flag, now threadbare, the once-gay colours washed out by age.

It was the flag of the 2nd Fifeshire Militia which was raised in St. Andrews in the days of Napoleon's threatened invasion. The flag was handed over in 1921 to the custody of the church, with impressive ceremony. It was brought from Alexandra Palace, under a full military escort. The 2nd Fifeshire was commanded by Col. Robert Anstruther, member of a well-known county family. The fugling staff of the battalion is in Edinburgh Museum.

More modern church ornaments and furnishings are a pulpit of Iona marble and a brass lectern, both given in memory of a distinguished minister of last century, Dr. Boyd, known with affection and respect in the theological world as ' A. K. H. B.' The church is also a repository of memorials to the Fallen in the First and Second World Wars.

In recent years many of the gifts presented to the church have been for the express purpose of enhancing the beauty and dignity of the musical side of worship.

The records of the Kirk Session do not show the considerable discussions and ponderings that took place before they decided in 1882 to introduce instrumental music. Until then singing had been led by a precentor or singing master and the paid choir which he trained. First of all a harmonium was hired as an experimental measure, and then one was bought for £45.

Within recent years a much-appreciated gift was one of six bells to add to the original chime in order to raise it to the category of a full carillon. A skilled team of volunteer bell-ringers helps to accentuate the impressiveness of ceremonial occasions in the city as well as the religious services with their playing.

The beautiful organ now in the church was reconstructed fully in 1968 to make it one of the finest in the country, and at its console have sat the world's finest organists.

The Parish Church of the Holy Trinity to-day stands out in Scotland as a priceless heritage well worthy of an ancient city that is unsurpassingly rich in history and architecture.

Even its ample accommodation was being taxed in the early 19th century by the size of its congregations, and in 1839 the Church of St. Mary was erected in St. Mary's Place as an overflow from the Town Church. St. Mary's continued to serve this purpose for some 75 years, but after being disused for some years it was sold and converted into a Memorial Hall and meeting place for the local British Legion. They, in 1971 gifted it to the city for community purposes.

THE PARISH OF ST. LEONARD

The most recently erected church in St. Andrews came into existence in 1904. Its architecture, in Norman design, gives at a distance an impression of solid age far beyond its years. This is only fitting because the congregation of St. Leonard's has a remarkable history. Its origins can be traced far back in time, back almost to the introduction of Christianity into Scotland. The church had its beginnings in an ancient hospital or hospice that was maintained by the Culdees. In 1144 this hospice was transferred to the canons of the Augustinian Priory and by 1248 it was known by the name of St. Leonard, patron saint of prisoners and of travellers. It was an appropriate name for this resting place for pilgrims who had travelled far to the miraculous shrine containing the relics of St. Andrew. In origin the church was no more than a chapel attached to the hospice, but by 1413 it had quite clearly assumed the status of a parish church. When the hospice, in 1512 was converted into a college which ultimately became the College of St. Leonard the church was reconstructed and enlarged. This was necessary to accommodate the parishioners and the increasing number of college members.

When St. Leonard's College was abandoned in 1748, the college buildings were sold, but the university authorities retained the church ' in case it shall ever be repaired again and used as a church '. The remoteness of this possibility to the minds of the college authorities is indicated by their treatment of the fabric, as the bell-tower was demolished and the remainder of the building unroofed. It remained in this increasingly neglected condition until 1910. By then the congregation of St. Leonard's who had been given at the sale, the right of worship in the stately university chapel of St. Salvator, had left the university church and built their own new church of St. Leonard in the west end of the town, some distance removed from the boundaries of their ancient parish.

The present church was designed by Dr. McGregor Chalmers and dedicated in July, 1904. The stone was from the well-known local quarry of Nydie, Strathkinness. Its distinctly Norman design has Celtic motifs as decoration, giving the whole an appearance of well-constructed solidity, and yet of restfulness, as well as reminding of its ancient associations.

The old abandoned chapel of St. Leonard was partially restored in 1910, but its full reconstruction did not take place until 1948 when the fabric was put into a thoroughly sound condition. The restoration was a thoughtful plan of mediaeval design with a central screen that divides the building into a collegiate choir suitable for smaller academic services, and a nave that is used by the St. Leonard's parishioners for occasional services. Altogether it is a notable addition to the city's religious buildings, and a historic link in the congregation's records.

*   *   *   *   *   *   *   *

The other churches of the city provide an accurate mirror of Scotland's ecclesiastical history through the upheavals of its various phases following the Reformation. The few staunch Roman Catholics remaining in St. Andrews after that tremendous religious cataclysm did not dare, for countless generations, reveal their faith in concerted worship in the city that was once their capital. In fact, a Roman Catholic church was not again built until as recently as 1886 and it only came into existence because of the immense influence of the Marquess of Bute, Rector of the University. That, allied to his financial generosity, gave the courage and confidence to a tiny catholic community to build a place of worship once more in their former capital. It was an ugly structure of corrugated iron, far removed from the magnificence and splendour of early days.

By 1910 the congregation had gained sufficient strength and stature to secure a commanding site on the edge of the cliff at the Scores. So the present lovely little church, designed by Reginald Fairlie, came into existence.

STRIFE AND DISRUPTION

The pattern of history that sent Catholicism underground in the city after the Reformation was repeated some 140 years later with the abolition of Episcopacy in Scotland in 1689. It sent devout members of that faith into worshipping in a fearful secrecy, victims of petty persecutions and public derision, when they were not being denounced outright as traitors to their country.

As example, one, Margaret Skinner, bound herself under penalty of £100 sterling not to let her house as a meeting place for ' piscies '— then too closely allied with the Jacobites for safety. Her house has been identified as being at 42 South Street and in 1732 it was described as ' a very ordinary house, indeed, not pew'd.' One of the ill-starred Archbishop Sharp's grandsons generally stood at the door.

For many years successive generations of families congregated in secret in various places of a private nature for episcopal services, including for a time, Queen Mary's House and the old Hall of St. Leonards College. Another recorded meeting place was ' Tam Couper's big room ' in a house on the site of the present Town Hall. The episcopalians were still subject to many petty tyrannies until the dawn of the nineteenth century. By 1825 a climate of greater tolerance in the city allowed them to build a chapel ; and then the fine church at the foot of Queen's Gardens was erected in 1866 by Sir Rowand Anderson, a distinguished church architect. It is a handsome example of his work in the thirteenth century English style. Originally it featured a well-proportioned tower that was weakened by the storm of 1879 which brought down the first Tay Bridge. The tower ultimately had to be demolished in 1939 because of its defective foundations.

The little church of All Saints in North Castle Street, extremely picturesque and with interesting architectural features, was founded in very much the same way. A large hall and rectory are attached. It comes under the authority of the English Episcopal Church. Generous donors such as Dr. and Mrs James Younger of Mount Melville contributed to it.

What might best be termed the modern churches of the city serve as monuments erected in the last century to the strongly-held religious views of stubborn-minded Scots who resolutely refused to accept various of the edicts of the Established Church of Scotland. They round off and bring up-to-date the ecclesiastical history of St. Andrews and of Scotland.

Abolition of the Episcopal prelacy in 1689 was followed by the Reform Church of Scotland becoming free and autonomous within its own sphere for the first time. The subsequent Act of Union provided that the Presbyterian Church should become the national Church of Scotland, and in the course of the eighteenth century the Established Church underwent a gradual process of far-reaching change. At first the effects of the national poverty of the times were everywhere apparent. Churches generally were poor and unimpressive in architecture. The minister of a church was subject to the

99

watchful scrutiny of his kirk session whose members took their duties with inordinate seriousness. In some areas, and St. Andrews was no exception, elders themselves, as we have already recorded, went forth in search of offenders against the church's laws. The Sabbath was a day of forbiddingly austere solemnity and during this early period of the Established Church Calvanism hardened and distorted pitilessly the great doctrines of the faith. The Holy Willies of Robert Burns were in their element.

Only later on in the century did a more humane and sympathetic evangelical appear. Until the Patronage Act of 1732 dissenters were a negligible element in Scottish Church life. It was from the tyranny of that measure a myriad schisms were produced. The Associated Presbytery of Dissenters was formed ; in due course the Relief Church was founded. The seceders displayed fanatic zeal, but no co-operation among themselves. They were split into splinter movements ; Burghers, Anti-Burghers ; Auld Lichties, New Lichties ; Wee Frees, Lifters and Anti-Lifters. All formed themselves into tiny congregations to worship in their own way, aloof from the Established Church and from each other.

St. Andrews had its full share of them. In the city the influence and spirit of the seceders lingered long and it was their tenacity and example that laid the foundations of three new church buildings erected in the nineteenth century that survive and prosper to-day, two of them again within the fold of the Church of Scotland.

Hope Park Church, standing conspicuously on the corner of St. Mary's Place, was built in 1865, a gracious example of Victorian church architecture. Its founders were early seceders from the Established Church. The congregation was first associated with the Burgher branch of the Secession Church. Its original meeting place was a barn in one of the old Scottish ' closes ' off South Street, known as Imrie's Close. This barn served as their church for 25 years from 1749 and in that time the congregations were subjected to many annoying practical jokes by students of the university. They removed ultimately to an old building in another close, also in South Street, and remained there for fifty years. This is the wide entry at 141 South Street, still known as the Burghers' Close. The expanding congregation moved to a third building, this time in North Street. It served for forty years until it, too, became too small, and the present fine church was brought into being.

100

The congregation were known during this long period variously as the Burghers, the United Secession, United Presbyterian, United Free, until in 1929 Hope Park came into the fold of the Church of Scotland. Its history is, in essence, the history of much of the Scottish Church since 1689.

Similarly the Martyrs' Church, almost opposite University Chapel in North Street, was originally a Free Church and then a United Free before also entering the Church of Scotland. Its foundation was 1843 and the congregation's first place of worship was opened following the Disruption. A plain and undistinguished building, it was demolished in 1925 to make way for the present structure which is unobtrusive, but pleasing to anyone who shows the perspicacity to give it a close inspection.

(*University photograph*).
St. Leonard's Chapel, a mouldering ruin until its reconstruction in 1952.

Harbour on a quiet summer morning, with leisure boats supplanting commerce.

SCOTLAND'S FINEST TOWN PORT

" Ane cumlie and Perfite Pend "

(*Martine*)

A COMMANDING architectural feature of the city, the embodiment of history, is the ancient gateway to South Street that once marked the western limit of the community. The Westgait or West Port, so aptly described above by Fordun ; ' The Port ' to generations of citizens ; a heritage from their forefathers and a part of their lives as much as the sands, the cliffs and the links.

The survival of this, one of only two town gateways remaining in Scotland, and much the better preserved, is probably explained by the fact that it was reconstructed in 1589 as a copy of Edinburgh's Netherbow Port, long since vanished. It was built to be impressive, while the other town ports of Mercatgait, and at either end of Swallowgait were of relatively plain form, similar to the surviving Sea Port in the Priory Wall facing the harbour. The 1589 work was a reconstruction of an earlier gate in a more elaborate form, which occupied the site. This replaced the original west port of the twelfth century, built further east and known as the Southgait. The Blackfriars Monastery was adjacent, but stood just outside the town, as was the practice of that order. It was in 1838, with the disappearance of the Northgait Port that the West Port became the sole remaining ancient city gate.

In 1843 the ' Port ' was extensively renovated as part of Provost Playfair's plans to improve the town. The sculptured panel that represents the arms of King David I in whose reign the Royal Burgh was founded, was placed on the west face at that time. The corresponding panel on the east face depicts the early representation of the city arms still perpetuated in the Town Hall.

As an ancient monument, and one of the finest in the country, the West Port has been taken into the responsibility of the Ministry of Works. At the ' Port ' the silver keys of the city were delivered to Charles II on his visit in 1650. The next occasion for such an event

H

did not take place until 1922 when the Prince of Wales, later King Edward VIII, received them when the freedom of the city was conferred on him, as well as the Captaincy of the Royal and Ancient Golf Club.   It is at this ancient gateway the students of the university still welcome their new Rector with a ceremonial address in Latin.

HARBOUR AND BAY

" The long sea rollers surge and sound "

(Lang)

At no time in its age-old existence has the ancient harbour of the city looked more picturesque than in the past few years when its commercial use has practically ceased.

It has ever provided a setting idyllically photogenic, and even centuries ago many illustrations depicting its waterfront scenes were produced.   Artists and camera-bearing tourists still find it alluringly depictable, particularly on Sunday mornings when the scarlet gowns of strolling students brighten the grey stones of the Long Pier.

This protective bastion against the sea's unceasing onslaughts has been demolished and re-built many times since the first harbourage was found by ancient fishermen at the Kinness Burn's mouth.

To-day, the Long Pier protects a few line net fishing boats and the varied small and colourful craft of a flourishing sailing club. Until only a few years ago the bay was considered too hazardous for sailing as a sport.   Its record of appalling fishing boat disasters and shipwrecks in the days before steam bear that out.   Yet, by enlisting all precautions, the sailing enthusiasts have established a successful and growing summer club.

Nowadays also, on the West Sands half a mile west of the harbour, the spectacular sport of land-sailing has found the ideal venue, fit for international events.

The earliest known date establishing the harbour's age is 1388 when Richard III of England commanded restitution to be made for the cargo from the vessel ' Le Clement ' which had been driven ashore off the Norfolk coast and plundered.   Piracy all round the coasts was a hazard of the early sailing vessels that used St. Andrews and other ports.   On one occasion two centuries later an English pirate ship was seized by avenging Fife sailors . . . . again off Norfolk. Of the crew of six captured four were hanged in St. Andrews and two at Anstruther.

105

One of the great storms that periodically rend the coast demolished the pier in 1655. Next year the timber and slates of the crumbling Castle were sold in order to help defray the expense of repairing it. Stones from the Cathedral were also used. The last extensive strengthening of the pier because of storm damage was in 1947. The harbour was at its busiest commercially last century when a large fishing fleet was supplemented by a prosperous coastal cargo trade.

The block of modern flats looming to-day over the harbour was reconstructed from an old warehouse and fisherfolk houses that bore the name of ' The Royal George ' after one of the first steamships. Behind it, Victorian iconoclasts built the town's first gasworks directly up against the Cathedral's precinct wall. This was only cleared away after well over a century of gross disfigurement of one of the city's finest scenes. The landscape to-day has been restored to something of its appearance in the pre-industrial era of last century's early years.

One feature that has departed forever is the ' quaint ' fishing quarter that clustered around the harbour, at the ' Royal George ' and at the clifftop at the Ladyhead, the name given to the east end of North Street. Although the Market Place was the traditional town centre, the tiny area around the Ladyhead formed the communal focus of interest for the burgh's fishermen. It had done so within records going back to the seventeenth century and no doubt for centuries before then. The fisher-folks were typical of the Scottish east coast communities to be found from Eyemouth up to John O' Groats. Snatching a perilous living from the sea they have always been self-contained, introvert little communities, mingling in St. Andrews practically not at all with the rest of the population, and little with other fishing villages.

Their world extended only from the harbour, up the cliffpath to the Ladyhead and their homes. Nets were mended and baited painstakingly outside their houses by the womenfolks, as the predatory gulls screeched endlessly around. Yet even on this tightly-knit group the spread of golf cast its influence. The fishermen found caddying and greenkeeping a less arduous and much less hazardous task than sweeping the offshore fishings in their tiny line boats. Caddying provided almost their only contact with the larger world outside for the men, and a means of escape for some. But for the women there

106

was no escape from the drudgery of eternal net-baiting, herring-gutting and fish-curing.

An even crueller slavery bound them before the fishermen were prevailed on to stop the practice of sending their wives and young children to gather mussels from the musselbeds or ' scalps ' as they are known locally, for bait. This was a freezing torture in soul-destroying conditions. The razor-sharp mussels and jagged rocks tore at benumbed hands while spray from the waves washed stinging brine into open cuts and wounds.

These mussel scalps formed for many generations one of the oldest and most remarkable industries in Scotland. The broad, shallow estuary of the River Eden was ideal for the ' planting ' and cultivation of mussels. This estuary was the chief source of bait for fishermen up and down the east coast, and consignments were regularly sold to other fishing villages. The scalps were run as a profitable community concern for hundreds of years and were a source of revenue to the Town Council itself which owned some of the mussel beds. Up until the beginning of the First War this slavery continued unabated and only when the beds became uneconomic for various reasons did it gradually die out. To-day, the mussel scalps are untended for the most part, despite occasional efforts to revive the trade.

The countless visitors to the town who admired the picturesque little houses of the fisherfolk in North Street and at the ' Royal George ' down at the harbour's edge, knew nothing of the conditions of grinding poverty and hardship they often concealed. The ' Royal George ' was a gaunt building, half warehouse, half a warren of fisher homes. With the fumes from the gasworks just behind ever-present, its own ugly building a scar on the lovely landscape provided by the Abbey Wall, the area of the ' Royal George ' was an example of Victorianism at its appalling worst. The gasworks were removed a number of years ago when the Ministry of Works made its usual skilled job of restoring the Abbey Wall and its surroundings to something of their former grandeur, while the skeleton walls of the ' George ' became the basis of the modern flats that now occupy the site.

The fishing community of St. Andrews no longer exists as such. Re-housing in other parts of the expanding town has dispersed its members in St. Andrews, and the few fishermen remaining are absorbed and integrated into the general population. Only fisher names such as Cunningham, Chisholm, Gourlay and a few others survive as reminders of the hardy fishermen and lifeboatmen of the past. They were men who daily as a matter of course braved the North Sea's terrors and who saved the lives of hundreds of sailors in the days before steam took much of the danger out of the currents and rocks of St. Andrews Bay.

The Bay has long been known and feared as one of the most treacherous waters around the Scottish coasts, and few stretches are more fiercely changeable. The Lifeboat Station in the days of sail was an important part of St. Andrews and was considered an essential service until the 1930s. Modern safety techniques have tamed the ferocity of the Bay to the extent that the flourishing sailing club has expanded in the past few years, a venture the fishermen of old would have condemned as foolhardy beyond belief. The harbour has been transformed into a gay and active recreational centre in the summer. The lobster pots and creels that once were everywhere are relegated to a corner and most of the quayside space is taken up with dinghy and yacht berths and a scattering of motorised pleasure boats, with the occasional canoe.

The winds of St. Andrews have also brought to the city in the last year or two a completely new sport. The West Sands have been found to be ideal for the exciting spectacle of sand-yacht racing to the extent that the British Championships have already been held on its broad and smooth stretch, with the prospect of even wider inter-national racing to come. The sand yachting authorities consider it to be one of the finest racing tracks in Europe.

AN ENTHRALLING HERITAGE

" And still St. Andrews Links with flags unfurled,
Shall peerless reign and challenge all the world."

(*Carnegie*)

IN the days when the quotation was first penned it may have sounded a trifle on the vainglorious side, but Carnegie's words have been justified by events as prophetic vision. The Links of St. Andrews reign supreme in golfing prestige by virtue of the fact that they have staged more major golfing occasions than any other British course, as well as being the oldest in the world.

So it is that during the period of an Open Championship, a Walker Cup contest or any other big international event, St. Andrews generates a highly-charged atmosphere of drama far removed from its everyday placid existence. An aura of tension pervades the air. It emanates in waves from the noted personalities of golf competing, and communicates itself to the fevered spectators milling frantically around the links, to overspill up into the town itself.

Even a non-golfing visitor in the streets who knows nothing of the game and its arenas . . . . and St. Andrews draws many such . . . . senses the mood and it draws him magnet-like to its source, the vicinity of the Royal and Ancient Clubhouse. He finds himself irresistibly sucked into a maelstrom of restless activity ; caught in a bewildering, almost hectic movement of sun-tanned competitors. The gladiators, taut-nerved and unseeing under the concentrated stare of wide-eyed wor-shippers, distraughtly killing time before going out to battle by way of the first tee ; their caddies, more relaxed, and enjoying openly the glamour of the occasion that falls vicariously on them according to the status of their player. A multitude of other figures builds up the scene, flamboyantly self-important, many of them because they know they are minor parts in it. There are the scurrying messengers, tapping telegraphists and the bustling reporters, all intent on their own parts. The commentating lords of the television towers capture their own considerable meed of awed interest, even more nowadays than the world's press golf writers, from a respectful and impressed public.

Around the eighteen holes of the arena with its international flags, marquees and tents, the walkie-talkie and the computer-type scoreboards have all been marshalled to ensure that the absorbing duels on the links are recorded and transmitted to the world news media. The clicking of cameras is constant in snatching a glimpse of the sporting celebrities of other spheres and all the public figures of numerous walks of life who have foregathered to see and to be seen.

The Royal and Ancient Golf Club has risen magnificently to a challenge that its original members could never have foreseen, of a fantastic escalation in golf's international popularity. They have organised in the alien atmosphere of a quiet little academic town, the spectacle of an Open Championship on the gigantic lines that are needed to satisfy the demands of the public. As impressarios of golf they have led the world.

For the seven days of a championship St. Andrews is transformed out of all recognition. And yet such gatherings are not new in the city's history. Half a millenium ago the world that was Europe thronged to its gates to trade at the Senzie Fair in the Priory a bare half mile away from the Links of Pilmuir.

What are those links ? This wasteland that is a priceless heritage in all that it has achieved for St. Andrews, the natal ground of this game that has swept the globe ?

The town links lie to the west of the old city. They comprise a rolling stretch of rough land whose vegetation is a mixture of thin turf, gorse, broom and bent grass that thrusts itself tenaciously and precariously up from a soil that is mostly sand and sea shell ; an area that has been an eternal battleground on which sea and land have striven for mastery for thousands of years.

Its links have been a valued possession to St. Andrews from the earliest days of a community existence. But, for the greater part of these centuries they were prized only because their scant produce helped to eke out the communal livelihood.

Certainly, as the records show, the game of golf had been played there before the fifteenth century. But the paramount benefit from possession of the land, granted by charter of King David I in 1123 was economic. The barren, windswept acres of the links supplied the townspeople and the clerics with peats for fuel ; turves for roofing the humble peasant houses. Rabbits were bred intensively by the

Priory's warrenders, and birds were snared and shot by all and sundry.

Attempts from time to time down the centuries to cultivate parts of the links failed ignominously.   After one such effort as recently as 1800, a husbandman chronicler scathingly recorded :—

> " The golfing course is a narrow strip of the Links which produces a species of herbage that is not good for animal except the rabbit.   This strip forms a hollow better supplied with moisture than the surrounding sand hillocks, and consequently furnished with a smoother kind of sod.   But, even this strip, which is the golfing ground, is better adapted for rabbits than for sheep."

That paragraph provides the key to the evolution of golf as a game.   It tells why the linksland that verges Scotland's east coastline beaches was ordained by Nature to become the birthplace of the game.

The 'species of herbage' referred to is fescue, a grass of the brome family that is a product of low fertility.   The single-bladed spikes of fescue band together into tiny but verdant patches, and in the less arid areas, into resilient turf.   This fescue weed, in other words, is the basic constituent of the best seaside links ;   the quirk of Nature that made possible the phenomenon of golf.

Another feature unique to St. Andrews of this pastime that has swept the world is that until 1894 anyone who cared ' to resort hither for the amusement of golf ' had the legal right to do so free of charge, whether inhabitant or stranger.   This privilege was continued to inhabitants alone up to as recently as 1946 when it required another parliamentary order to abolish free golf entirely.

Although its origins are shrouded in mystery, golf is generally conceded to be a form of the Dutch and Flemish Het Kolven, a ball-and-stick game that was played across country and on ice.   Breughel painted several pictures featuring the game.   It could well have been introduced to St. Andrews by the Flemish merchants who thronged to the ancient Senzie Fair (p. 55), at one time the largest of Scotland's ancient markets.   This was held annually in the grounds of the Augustinian Priory, the centre of the city's wealth from the 12th Century.

After the Reformation which so overwhelmingly affected the future of St. Andrews more than anywhere else in Scotland, the superiority (unconditional ownership) of the links passed to the Town. Had the community not possessed successive charters upholding its right to play golf there, and had the ground not proved incapable of cultivation, even this barren land might have been otherwise annexed. As it was, the Episcopal Archbishop Gladstanes confirmed all town rights in his charter dated 1610 which is still preserved.

The Roman-style Swilcan Bridge at the entrance to the Old Course, the most famous of the town's five golf courses, whose age is unknown, was not built for the convenience of golfers. It was part of the original route to the Links and to the Town's ancient harbour in the River Eden estuary where seals still sun themselves and dunlin and other marsh birds congregate in their thousands. ' *Herons, terns, and twittering, wheeling knots.*'

Historical records of St. Andrews life down the centuries are studded with passing references to golf being indulged in by citizens, students and their teachers. These have been dealt with at greater length in the author's ' Home of Golf ' which tells of the part played by St. Andrews men in making the game the world's most popular pastime. The records make mention of ball-makers and club-makers from the sixteenth century onwards. Early golf balls were made of wood, or flock encased roughly in leather ; later the manufacture of a ball called for a top hat-ful of boiled feathers. These were stuffed with an awl into a leather case which was sewn up. This was the ' featherie ', which was followed by the gutta-percha ball in 1848. Early golf clubs were fashioned by the skilled makers of bows and arrows, but only as a sideline. Later, the carpenters made clubs entirely of wood. Then blacksmiths started manufacturing clubs with heads of iron. Their purpose was to strike the ball out of awkward positions or ' lies ', because it was the cardinal rule of golf that the ball must be struck ' where it lies ', regardless of how difficult the situation.

BEGINNINGS OF SUCCESS

The first real impact of the game on the city's economy came when the Society of St. Andrews Golfers was formed. It formalised the rough-and-ready pursuit by adopting rules of play which had to be followed. Instead of players wandering thither and yon over the Links a directed ' course ' of nine holes out and back again was formed, with level patches, defined as ' green ' for the ' putting ' of the ball into a hole. Thus, a ' course ' became twice nine, or 18 holes, and the ' course ' itself became the golfing course.

From these meagre and unlikely beginnings the world-wide expansion of golf began. The game had always attracted in Scotland the enthusiasm of the landowners and noblemen, even of the great dignitaries of the Church, princes of the royal blood, and kings. The Royal Stuarts, many of them, were keen golfers. In and around Edinburgh James IV, even while issuing an edict to curtail the time-wasting sport, played it himself. James V also loved the game, and Mary, Queen of Scots, found pleasure in it.

Royal interest in golf persisted as players formed themselves into Clubs. William IV elevated the game by honouring it with his patronage when, in 1834, he allowed the Society of Golfers to assume the title of ' Royal and Ancient '. Since then prime ministers and royal princes have captained the R. and A. Club, including three uncles of Queen Elizabeth II. The Duke of Windsor was captain in 1922, his brother of York who became King George VI, in 1930, and the Duke of Kent in 1934.

From the early days after-golf conviviality was a concomitant of the game. In Regency times, the noblemen and landowners who played foregathered increasingly in the Black Bull Inn at the corner of South Street and Castle Street, and at Bailie Glass's famous hostelry ; enjoyed after a round, a heavy meal and heavier drinking, settled their bets for matches of the day and made more bets for the next day's games.

Later on, in 1835, the ' Society ' used the Union Parlour, conveniently adjacent to the Links. This was a Club or meeting place, founded for its members who were generally also members of the Archery and Golf Clubs. They also engaged cadets or ' caddies ' to carry their clubs. Many of these wealthy golfers built or bought houses in the town to pursue their pastime. The Society membership grew to a stage where they decided they must have a clubhouse entirely of their own. In 1854 the present clubhouse was built. Even by then, some of the Society's golfing customs had ripened into traditions.

The Spring and Autumn competitions of the original Society marking the opening and closing of the golfing season, soon assumed a considerable holiday significance for the townspeople and the golfers themselves. They assembled at the Tolbooth in Market Street. Then, in procession, the Captain and his supporters, preceded by the Town Crier, and followed by most of the town, marched down to the first tee, where under a battery of watchful, appraising eyes, the Captain played off. Only once was an attempt made to revive the Captain's procession from Town to Links. This was when St. Andrews held the inaugural ' Alcan ' tournament of champions in 1967. But, *autres temps, autres modes*, the spectators were almost as embarrassed at the parade as were the famous professionals roped in to take part in it. The simple pleasures and excitements of 150 years ago of a procession and a band proved too unsophisticated for these present more *blasé* days.

In the early days the captaincy was won in competition, but later, as the office gained considerably in prestige, the Captain was elected. He played himself into office by a formal drive, hit—or mis-hit, according to skill, from the first tee. The caddie who retrieved his ball and brought it back to him was rewarded by the Captain with a golden sovereign. That tradition, with the help of the Royal Mint, which strikes an occasional few golden sovereigns, continues to-day, each September.

SIGNIFICANT CHANGES

Significant changes took place in the game from 1800 onwards. The gutta ball, first made in 1848, brought the cost of golf within the range of small purses. Artisans, or tradesmen, began to play. Caddies were mostly farm labourers, fishers or the poorer artisans. They themselves became highly skilled in the game, and formed their own clubs, of which the most famous is the St. Andrews Golf Club, founded in 1843. From their ranks came the first professionals. Of these, the best-known are Allan Robertson, the first professional golfer, Old Tom Morris and his son, ' Young Tommy ', the most celebrated golfer of the 19th century. Old Tom came in time to symbolise all that was finest in the game of golf and best in the Scottish character. The professionals, playing for big money stakes, attracted enthusiastic and highly partisan spectators to their individual matches.

Soon, their services were in demand to teach the game over a wider area of Scotland, into England, and finally, overseas. St. Andrews over the past century has sent hundreds of its sons as professionals and greenkeepers to every corner of the globe.

The wealthy golfers of the R. and A. also carried the love of their sport with them on their travels, and so golf was introduced over the world. As the fascination and fast-growing popularity of the game spread, St. Andrews has come to be venerated as the ' Home of Golf ' and the centre of an almost poetic mystique that has always been invested in the game. This includes an expanding literature in verse and prose extolling its pleasures, and an esoteric language that surrounds its play. The start of that literature was a treatise written in 1687 . . . ' The onlie way of playing at the Golfe '. Many homely nineteenth century Lowland Scots words on golf have passed into international use.

All this had a cumulatively beneficial effect on the city.

From being a somewhat eccentric local pastime in its earlier days golf emerged not merely as a sport but as a social phenomenon. A true picture of the St. Andrews of to-day cannot be obtained by the visitor without bearing that fact in the forefront of his mind.

By the time they came to be written in 1885, the words of R. F. Murray, an American poet studying at St. Andrews University, were literally true :

"Would you like to see a city taken over,
Mind and body by a tyrannising game."

They contained not a whit of poetic license, but had been a statement of fact for many years. The old and the young, high and lowly, had become bound together in a common interset that was powerful enough to breach the barriers of the rigid Victorian caste system. Rich and poor, the laird and his tenant, played together. They discussed golf, sought to teach its technique to each other, and they wrote poems and panegyrics about it. The annals of the game were meticulously recorded ; its champions were hero-worshipped. It was all-absorbing, as for its devotees, it continues.

From the first days of competitive play, beginning with the emergence of the first professional golfer, Allan Robertson of St. Andrews, an aura has always surrounded its champions. Their pedestal has stood higher than that in any other sport. In St. Andrews, the first to experience this as its entire community surrendered to a magnificent obsession, two men have stood out, elevated to an almost idolatrous level.

The idol of the 19th century was ' Young Tommy ', the son of Tom Morris, the St. Andrews greenkeeper who later became professional to the Royal and Ancient Golf Club, and known the world over as the ' Grand Old Man of Golf.' Tom Morris, the elder, survived his brilliant son by over thirty years, for Young Tommy died tragically at the age of 24 and at the height of his golfing fame. All the ingredients of high melodrama were stirred into the brief story of his life.

He won his first prize money at the age of 16 years and went on to annex the Open Championship Belt four times in a row by the time he was 21. Then, in the greatest days of his golfing triumph, tragedy struck the handsome and modest champion. He lost his young wife and babe in childbirth. He himself died, a few months later, in December, 1875.

Young Tommy, a target of adulation in his lifetime, became a legendary figure in death, the most noted golfer of the 19th century. Players from all over the world contributed to the memorial stone that marks his grave in the quiet Old Cemetery of St. Andrews in the shadow of the Cathedral. His memory is still cherished a century later.

The 20th century parallel to Young Tommy Morris was Bobby Jones of Atlanta, U.S.A.—ever associated with St. Andrews although an American. A dignified, almost austere figure even before tragedy came to him also, to consign him to an invalid's chair for many years, Jones preferred to be known everywhere as ' Bob '. Everywhere, that is, except St. Andrews. There, he well knew, the Scottish diminutive was a mark of distilled affection and respect, and not of public familiarity. The famous golfer who, in 1930, performed the feat, never again likely to be equalled, of winning the British and American ' Open ' and Amateur Championships in one year, had a special relationship with the little grey Scottish town by the sea. It was his spiritual home ; ' I could take out of my life everything except my experiences at St. Andrews and I would still have had a rich and full life,' he told the world.

At a unique ceremony in the University's graduation hall which was crowded with the world's greatest golfers of the day, he was presented in October, 1958 with the freedom of the City of St. Andrews, the second American to be so honoured. The first was 18th century scientist, Benjamin Franklin. By the time of his honour Bobby Jones had retired more than twenty years from the golfing scene, but to St. Andrews his deeds and his personality were just as memorable ' as if it had been but yesterday ', as a noted golfing journalist re-

116

ported.   His death in 1971 was the occasion some months afterwards for a notable commemoration service at St. Andrews when the Town Church of the Holy Trinity was not spacious enough to hold the distinguished gathering who came to honour him, ' A golfer matchless in skill and chivalrous in spirit.'

This nineteenth century phenomenon of golf as a social force has perhaps never been more strikingly exemplified than in the life of Tom Morris, the elder.   A humble son of the soil whose chief qualities apart from his skill in the game, were his natural kindliness of nature and his native courtesy, he was respected throughout his life, revered in his later years, and sought out by the greatest in the land. In a long and sometimes tragic life, Tom had acquired a sustaining philosophy.   This he revealed in the course of a New Year Day talk in 1886 at the age of 65, with A. J. Balfour, the famous politician.

' Had it not been for golf ', he told the future Prime Minister of Britain, in his native Fife dialect, ' I'm not sure that at this day I would have been still a living man.   I've had my troubles like the rest, and my sorrows, so that at times to lie down and die looked all that was left in life for me.   It was as if the very soul had gone out of me.   But, with the help of God and of golf, I have managed to survive.   (' Wi' the help o' God, an' o' gowff, I've gotten warsled through somehoo or ither.')

Perhaps the theme of these thoughts conveyed in the home-spun language of his native town to a great statesman who was to him a fellow golfer in whom to confide, contains the reason for the world-wide popularity of this game with which St. Andrews will be forever associated : that on the golf courses of the world, besetting troubles are, for the time being, banished.   The latest to discover this is the Japanese nation, fervent converts to the game.   One of its notable sons, Zenya Hamada, has honoured St. Andrews and the game by founding the ' New St. Andrews Golf Course ' in his country.   He has also made a supremely generous gift in acknowledgment, to ' the Home of Golf '.

DISTINCTIVE ATMOSPHERE

The golfing scene in St. Andrews to-day then, is permeated with a distinctive atmosphere that derives in great measure from the traditions and story of the past.   It has become once again a shrine—not

117

of a religion, but of a sport ! But its world-wide attraction also owes considerably to two unique features in the annals of the game.

The first is the Royal and Ancient Golf Club whose presence, as we have already emphasised, has contributed everything to the little city's eminence in the game and much to its latter-day prosperity.

The famous Old Course is the other. The association of the R. and A. with the Old Course began with the Club's formation in 1754. That association later raised St. Andrews to its undreamed international fame in golf above other Scottish places where it had also been played for centuries, such as Musselburgh, Leith, Perth, and in the west, Prestwick. It is an unusual relationship. The Society of St. Andrews Golfers, as the R. and A. were first known, had its nucleus in noblemen and landowners who played the little-known game in the Edinburgh vicinity. For various reasons, early in the eighteenth century they elected to transfer their allegiance to the superior and much quieter Links of St. Andrews.

The Society flourished in the next hundred years and its members found themselves being hailed as its arbitrators and leaders by the numerous new clubs coming into existence all over the country. No doubt this attitude was influenced to a great extent by the fact that the Society had been accorded in 1834 the unique privilege of Royal patronage. It became the august Royal and Ancient Golf Club which has ever since exercised a benevolent authority over the game.

But the R. and A. possessed neither a clubhouse nor a golf course of its own ! The clubhouse, built in 1854, provided magnificent facilities and comforts then that are now regarded as commonplace. It is one of the most-photographed buildings in the world and exclusively a male sanctuary. Its trophy rooms contain treasures and mementos of the game that are irreplacable. Most important of all, from its offices the rules of golf are administered and the annual British Open Championships organised.

Yet the Old Course, which the clubhouse overlooks and where the Club's own competitions are played, does not belong to the R. and A. but to the townspeople of St. Andrews ! An Order of Parliament outlines and protects certain club privileges. The situation is unique but it has obtained with outstanding success ever since the Club came into existence. There seemed no reason why it should not continue indefinitely, although the Reorganisation of

118

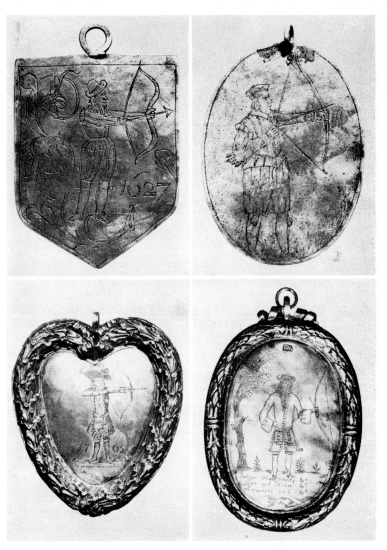

Four of the 17th and 18th Century medals presented by winners
of the Silver Arrow.

(*University photograph*).

Vaulted refectory of Deans Court, former 16th Century mansion,
now a post-graduate residence.

(*University photograph*).

Sketch of the new Students' Union on the central site of West Park Hotel.

Local Government has posed a considerable problem, with the acquisition of all burghal property by the new Regional Authority. Throughout more than two hundred years compromise and expedient have played their part in successive agreements between the Town and the R. and A. Now a new agreement must be reached under the new Statute.

That document must be one which, in the national interest, protects the Royal and Ancient Club's prestige and position in golf that is bound up with the Old Course of St. Andrews ; one that must not jeopardise the city's reputation as the Mecca and Home of Golf. Golfing history apart, both are invaluable assets to Scotland's tourist industry.

The Old Course is to-day only one of five golfing circuits that have been fashioned out of the town's links, including a recent nine-hole course. With the game's soaring popularity there has been initiated a pattern of innovations to suit modern conditions and the needs of ever-increasing hordes of spectators. Yet, the ' Old ' is still in feature and characteristic the ' course ' that was mapped out in 1820. Before then there was no ' course ' to follow ; players just wended their way back and forth as they pleased.

Many important relics of early golf have been spirited overseas to museums, particularly in America. The most treasured and significant fortunately remain with the important museum in the R. and A. Those numerous players who find their interest in golf history cannot fail to be fascinated by another golf museum in the town. This is a highly unusual exhibition of golf clubs, balls, photographs and illustrations that is a feature of the old established clubmaking firm owned by Laurie Auchterlonie, honorary professional of the R. and A. The Auchterlonie collection is by far the most complete record of the evolution of golfing implements in the world. Its historic importance is immense. It is the centrepiece of the Pinehurst World Hall of Fame Museum, North Carolina, of which Laurie Auchterlonie has been appointed honorary curator.

Altogether, in introducing this primitive pastime and converting it into a world-wide sport, St. Andrews has earned a unique international prestige to-day.

The prosperity of the city to-day probably rests more firmly on the last of the three pillars of its fame, of History, Learning and Golf.

THE UNIVERSITY — TO-DAY

" Towers that the salt winds vainly beat "

(Lang)

WITH its ancient tower thrusting high above the surrounding architectural conglomerate, the 15th Century Collegiate Church of St. Salvator, which is the hub of the University of St. Andrews, surely represents the fulfilment of a romantic's dream of a seat of learning.

But a span of almost six centuries of history has contained little of romance. The fate of the University has been an incessant struggle for survival that has never been fought more successfully than in the present dynamic era.

The ancient buildings in the Old Town to-day are only a small part of the expanded and rejuvenated University of St. Andrews that has arisen during the past few years.

In 1967 Queen's College, Dundee, an integral part of the St. Andrews University from its founding as University College, Dundee, in 1881, was severed to become the nucleus of Dundee University. St. Andrews found itself in a critical position. Shorn and denuded, it was the smallest although the oldest centre of higher learning in Scotland. Its remaining students numbered only a scant 1,700, a number too small for St. Andrews to remain a viable, independent university.

Its administrators, headed by their new Principal, Dr. J. Steven Watson, were presented in that year of 1967 by the Government with an expansionist policy that was dictated by the demands of a post-war technological upsurge. It sought to thrust the direction of the ancient university into unvisualised channels. The loss of Queen's College deprived St. Andrews of five faculties and half of its endowments. The number of students remaining was insufficient to enable the existing departments to operate with full efficiency. Two new Chairs, Psychology and Fine Arts, were established as a start, and a number of other Chairs have been added since. The University Court embarked on an ambitious programme, prompted by the U. G. C., to expand to some 3600 students as a ceiling figure. This

121

was 1969-70. Despite discouraging and disheartening fluctuations in Government grants, the expansion has been extraordinarily dynamic. It marks the period as the most stimulating and notable in the venerable existence of the University.

This remarkable growth could never have been made possible without the acquisition by the University authorities of the key area of ground on the city's western perimeter known as the North Haugh. It was secured from the neighbouring Strathtyrum estate, to open up a vista of one of the finest and most spacious university campuses in Britain. On it were erected, as a start, a new Physics Department, followed by Mathematics and Chemistry Buildings. At the western corner Andrew Melville Hall, an unorthodox open-plan residence for men and women students, was also built. Ample space remains for later extensions and new buildings planned. The site links up to the south with the university playing fields and other student residences, old and new, including University Hall and the David Russell group of residences.

This period of almost hectic expansion was preceded by a longer-planned series of extensions beginning around 1960. They included the Buchanan Building in the city centre, other student residences that were built or secured by property purchase, and the magnificent central West Park site that was bought for a new Student Union. Equally central, St. Katharine's School was purchased in 1971 as the site for a new University Library to replace the South Street building, long since taxed beyond its capacity. The site, almost contiguous with the St. Salvator's College buildings, will also accommodate an Arts Centre and the Department of Fine Arts and Psychology.

Altogether the surging expansion of the University in the succeeding years has not merely survived the severance of Dundee, but has considerably increased the number of students at St. Andrews.

Further ambitious plans are pending to bring the numbers up to the desired 3600, and the pace of their progress will depend on the availability of Government grants.

The University is at one with the municipal authorities in desiring in this future expansion, to maintain that distinctive character of St. Andrews which has been its eternal charm. That includes ensuring that St. Andrews remains the only completely university city in Britain.

122

The clearly defined policy laid down by the University Senate by which its future is to be shaped, is that St. Andrews shall remain essentially a small and individual university, in balance and in harmony with the ancient city. St. Andrews will be unique in Scotland, if not in Britain, in that its ceiling student population of around 3600 students at the end of a fifteen year phased development will be lodged very largely in accommodation provided by the University. This includes orthodox residence for over 1750 students and also groups of flats to hold another 600. These flats are a new feature of student life. They will be built in different areas of the town, being based for meals on the conventional residences nearby, and linked to them.

This relative smallness in numbers will have the effect of retaining St. Andrews as a compact and closely-knit unit University that will be distinguished from the main body of British academic life by two unique features. The first is that outside Cambridge and Oxford, St. Andrews will stand alone in being almost completely residential.

Secondly, it has been made possible to continue the development of a system of tutorial teaching that is traditional in the university.

THE MEDIAEVAL UNIVERSITY

THE fortunes of the city's university, from its foundation in 1413, have followed a course that has been roughly parallel with those of the town itself.

Both Town and Gown owe their existence to the influence of the Church. It was destined to be one of the greatest privileges ever bestowed on St. Andrews when scholars of the Augustinian Priory felt impelled to initiate a seat of learning which was to develop into the first university in Scotland. It came into being as part of a movement which established national universities in many of the kingdoms of Europe in the fourteenth and fifteenth centuries.

In Scotland this development was accelerated not only by the growth of national feeling but to some extent at least by the highly individual course pursued by the Scots in the Great Schism of the Papacy (1378-1418). The Priors, about 1410, established a school for higher studies and the society of masters and scholars received formal incorporation in terms of a charter granted by Bishop Wardlaw. Many of these scholars had studied in the European universities, particularly those of France, and the constitution of St. Andrews was founded on that of Orleans and certain other French universities in which the dominance of the teaching masters, unquestioned at Paris and Oxford, was modified by the authority of the Bishop-Chancellor, and by the participation of all members of the academic society in the election of its administrative head, the Rector. As Chancellor, the Bishop of St. Andrews—and Archbishop from 1472—exercised a general supervision over the University and conferred degrees on candidates examined and attested by the Dean and masters of the appropriate faculty—Arts, Theology or Canon Law.

One of the chief considerations at the time of initiation was the stirring in Scotland of Lollardy, the heretical movement organised in England by Wycliffe, that presaged Reformation. It had to be combatted. Therefore, Bishop Henry Wardlaw successfully interceded with Rome in favour of the project and the Papal bulls were issued in 1413. These were duly promulgated in February of the following year with considerable ceremony in the refectory of the Priory.

The oldest object in the University is the matrix of the University Seal. This must have been cut before 1418 because it bears the arms of the antipope Benedict from whom the University transferred its allegiance in that year.

Almost as old are the three mediaeval maces around the older two of which exists a mystery of identification. Which is the mace of the Faculty of Arts and which belongs to the Faculty of Canon Laws ? Thousands of graduates have seen the six beautiful maces owned by the University, three of them modern. They appear on ceremonial occasions. There is nothing quite like them in Britain, apart from the single Glasgow University mace. The older foundations of Oxford and Cambridge have no treasures to bear comparison with these three mediaeval maces of St. Andrews.

The mace of St. Salvator's College was made by the founder of the College, Bishop Kennedy, in 1461, and its design bears only a very general resemblance to that of the other two which are older. In the records the three were variously referred to as ' silver staves ', ' beadle wands ', or simply ' honours of the University ', but doubt exists as to which of the older two is which. Before 1892 the mace ornamented with six shields was regarded

124

as that of the Faculty of Canon Laws and the other as belonging to the Faculty of Arts. In that year A. J. S. Brook, an Edinburgh silversmith argued that the Faculty of Arts had a mace in 1418 ; that the mace with shields was clearly about that date and that therefore it was the mace of the Faculty of Arts.

R. N. Smart of the University Library in an article some years ago suggested that Brook was wrong in his identification and that the traditional one was correct. He argues that the real Arts mace was almost certainly made in Scotland and was actually finished in St. Andrews. The other was of Parisian workmanship and could not be the Arts mace. The Scottish-made one was probably copied from the other and can only be dated as before 1457. An element of intriguing doubt must always remain on the subject, just as mystery surrounds a number of St. Andrews relics of the distant past.

The three modern maces were added during the present century. The earliest was presented in 1912 to University College, Dundee, and it passed to the University of Dundee in 1967. Another was presented anonymously to the School of Medicine of the University. In 1958 a mace was secured for the University as a whole, as distinct from its constituent parts. It was designed and wrought in London, the head taking the form of a figure of St. Andrew, modelled on the celebrated painting by El Greco. In the possession of these six symbolic maces alone, the University of St. Andrews is uniquely endowed in the world's academic history.

St. Salvator's College possessed other treasures, but it seems to have been singularly unfortunate in its eighteenth century professors. In addition to destroying unnecessarily the roof of the ancient chapel, they sold in 1747 for melting down, the historic silver belonging to the College. Such an act seems negligent of the College interests beyond belief, and the use of the money for the purpose of repairing the temporary college buildings of St. Leonard's College is equally incredible.

Among valuable University silver remaining is the St. Mary's mazer, the earliest fully-marked piece of Scottish silver ; the St. Mary's College Salt, the Guild Cup also from St. Mary's, and some equally fine pieces from St. Leonard's College including an early mazer. Particularly important historical collections exist in some of the departmental museums. They include early scientific instruments, together with the clocks in the Library obtained by the

125

noted astronomer, James Gregory, for use in the observatory at the top of Dyers Brae which was destined never to be completed.

Thus the first Scottish university was formally inaugurated, but it was a university without buildings. Makeshift accommodation was first acquired in 1419, the so-called Chapel of the College of St. John the Evangelist in South Street on the site of the University Library. This was no more than a small chantry college adapted to support masters of the Faculty of Theology and Arts and to provide accommodation for their lectures and meetings.

Then, in 1430, as the academic atmosphere warmed and expanded, Bishop Wardlaw next founded the Pedagogy on a site immediately to the west of St. John's for the Faculty of Arts. The Pedagogy soon absorbed its older neighbour and endured for rather more than a hundred years until it in turn was absorbed by St. Mary's College in 1540 when the combined sites of St. John's and the Pedagogy passed to the new foundation.

But the first university buildings to be erected in Scotland as such were the College and Church of St. Salvator founded by Wardlaw's successor, Bishop James Kennedy, for the study of Arts and Theology. This facade of church and tower that adorns and enriches the North Street we know to-day, was conceived on a splendid scale, but Kennedy may have found difficulty in carrying through his original plan. At any rate, the structure was still incomplete at his death in 1465, but it was the first fully organised and endowed collegiate society to be established in Scotland. To-day the focal point of the University of St. Andrews, the magnificent Collegiate Church still forms the principal place of academic worship in St. Andrews, and is generally regarded as one of the finest and most interesting of British mediaeval creations. Countless generations of teachers, students and visitors have come to worship under its roof and have gazed down on the battered tomb of Bishop Kennedy in the awe-inspiring knowledge that there lie the remains of the greatest Scotsman of his age. He not only erected the first university building in Scotland but directed the path of higher education that the rest of the nation would later follow.

The tower of St. Salvator's steeple was originally flat-topped and it was used by the French in 1548 as a gun emplacement to bombard the nearby Castle (p. 81). In the next hundred years and up to the

126

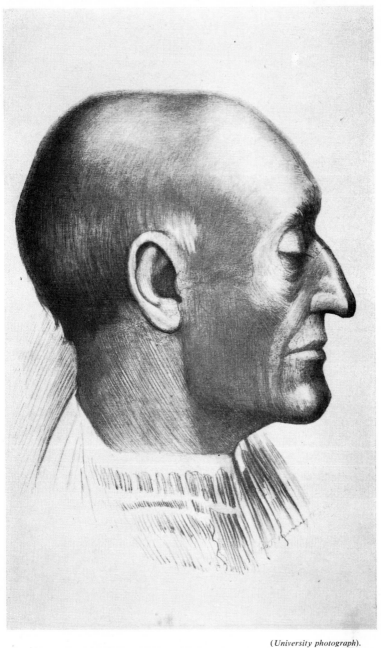

Bishop James Kennedy, founder of the College of St. Salvator. A sketch
made from the reconstruction of his skull.

Classical lines of the steeple of St. Salvator's.

Reformation, the religious revolution that convulsed and transformed Scotland, many additions were made to St. Salvator's, but the original street frontage of splendid tower and collegiate church remains intact. Even after the many changes inevitable in an existence of over 500 years the Collegiate Church of St. Salvator is one of the finest examples of Gothic art in Scotland. The present stone spire was added by Archbishop Hamilton, the last of the pre-Reformation Catholic primates in Scotland.

Although stripped two centuries ago of its massive vaulted roof, an acoustical failure, the College Chapel is superb still. But gone are the panoplied vestments of the days of Catholic splendour ; vanished most of them, in the general sacking that immediately followed on the Reformation. Fortunately, the beautifully ornate mace, fashioned in Paris in 1461 and the gift of Kennedy, and Katharine's Bell, associated now with the students' Kate Kennedy pageant, remain as direct links with the days of the university's foundation.

Of many ' restorers ' of the Collegiate Church, Dr. Reginald Fairlie in the present century, R. G. Cant considers, has been the most successful. Bishop Kennedy's tomb, although badly mutilated by the fall of the vaulted roof, is the finest of its kind in the country and a fitting monument to this outstanding Scotsman of his century.

In the last century Principal J. D. Forbes from 1859 to 1868 was deeply interested in a project to restore the College Chapel. In a memoir to his work on the Chapel Principal Shairp, his successor, gives a vivid description of the interior over a century ago. " The original roof, he states in 1873, is said to have been of a peculiar and rare construction—massive blue stone, deeply engroined. Within the chapel is the tomb of the founder, a Gothic structure, wrought in Paris, of blue stone, in the middle of the fifteenth century, which originally must have been of wonderful beauty, since even in its cruel defacement it still shows so fair. As the old stone roof is said to have been nearly flat, Professors about a hundred years since either conceived themselves, or were persuaded by some architect that it would one day fall in and crush them. They therefore resolved to have it removed and a common lath and plaster ceiling placed in its stead. So solidly, however, was the old roof compacted that the workmen in order to remove it, had to detach it from walls and buttresses and let it fall en masse. The fall is said to have shaken the whole city. But however this may be, it is only too certain that it shattered the richly wrought columns, canopies and pinnacles of the founder's tomb.

" A maimed and mutilated fragment that tomb now stands, beautiful still in its decay, proving that professors of the eighteenth century could be more ruthless and insensible to beauty than were the ruder Reformers of the sixteenth or seventeenth.

" But besides the mutilated tomb of which no restoration was possible, parsimony and Philistinism had combined to make the rest of the church hideous. High bare pews, an unsightly gallery at one end, lath plaster and whitewash, floods of harsh light from many windows—ugliness could go no further.

" To the removal of these deformities and the restoration of the church, Forbes gave his undivided attention for one whole winter. At his earnest advocacy a more liberal Government undertook to restore the whole body of the church, and what with seemly oaken seats, a raftered roof, and more appropriate mullions and tracery in the old pointed windows, the work has been done so as to render the College Church, if not so perfect as might have been desired, a great improvement on what it was. By his solicitations the College and private persons were stirred up to substitute for the former common glass with its untempered garishness, new painted windows which by toning down the light gave at least solemnity to the church. As a result of all these exertions the College Church, if it has not re-attained its pristine beauty, has certainly lost its former repulsiveness." St. Andrews undoubtedly owes much to Principal Forbes.

Another, but lesser-known memorial is the sculptured slab consisting of a bronze casting in a frame of Greek Tinos marble to Andrew Lang, the poet and historian whose student days at his alma mater were the theme of much of his verse.

A pulpit from which, some say, John Knox preached in Holy Trinity Church while he was in St. Andrews has an honoured place in St. Salvator's. As craftsmanship of the late 16th Century, it is well worthy of preservation, although experts place it as having been fashioned after Knox's time at Holy Trinity. This pulpit was discarded by the Town Church session at the time of the restoration of 1798, which would seem to bear out that view. Had it been a link with Knox it would almost certainly have been retained.

The fact that the College of St. Salvator was a later, and separate institution of the University, occasioned a bitter rivalry with the struggling Pedagogy of St. John, which had always been insufficiently endowed. This led to at least one warlike confrontation when the

St. Salvator men actually assaulted their opponents with bow and arrow.

Scholars, no less than churchmen, were warlike individuals in those days !

COLLEGE OF ST. LEONARD

A historically appropriate site was chosen in 1512 by Prior John Hepburn, builder of the Abbey Wall, along with Archbishop Alexander Stewart for the addition of a third appendage to the university, in the College of St. Leonard. Alexander Stewart, incidentally was in the line of warlike church leaders who were as much at home with the sword as the breviary, and he died at Flodden. His tomb is in St. Leonard's Chapel.

Within the Priory grounds stood an ancient hospice that had been maintained by the Culdees for the benefit of pilgrims and poor people. It was taken over by the Augustinians in 1144. The chapel attached to the hospice became in 1413 the Parish Church of St. Leonard. The chosen site for the new college was historically appropriate because it was there that the masters and students of learning within the Priory had foregathered as the nucleus of what would, in time, become a university.

Men of outstanding scholarship and religious leaders quickly made St. Leonard's famous and it produced many distinguished figures, the most illustrious of them being, possibly George Buchanan, whose reputation was high in Europe as a humanist and scholar. St. Leonard's became the birthplace of the Reformation in Scotland and was the spiritual home of such as Wishart and John Knox. It attracted the sons of the most powerful nobles in Scotland.

Indeed, St. Leonard's goes even deeper into the roots of university history. It was originally a hospice maintained by the ancient Culdees before being taken over by the Augustinians in 1144. They gave it the name of St. Leonard, the patron saint of the poor.

The University prospered in those early days of St. Leonard's, despite warlike times that were not at all conducive to the placid pursuit of learning. From 1544 until 1550 the city of St. Andrews lay almost continuously under the threat of the English invasion. In 1546-47, when Norman Leslie's band of Protestants assassinated Cardinal Beaton (p. 78), they occupied his castle which came under long and heavy siege.

129

The situation became so serious, with Leslie's predatory band making regular forays from the Castle to plunder the town, that the university, for safety, was withdrawn for a time to the seclusion of the Archbishop's palace at Monimail, some twelve miles distant. Thence, significantly, the faculty hoods and maces were among the valuables removed. The strategic use of cannon from the University tower by French artillery sent to bolster the Catholic Church finally helped to dislodge Leslie's band from the Castle, and to send their preacher, John Knox, to two years in the French galleys.

But the Reformation, with its tremendous impact on the University no less than the city, was close at hand.

So, there was seen yet again the continuing thread of irony in the history of St. Andrews in the fact that St. Leonard's, the birthplace of the Reformation suffered most in the decline that followed it. In the necessary amalgamation of St. Salvator's and St. Leonard's Colleges, it was the latter whose buildings were swallowed up and sold, although they were in better condition. Its wealth was annexed and its prestige vanished in this ' takeover ' of 1747, deplored so bitterly by Samuel Johnson when he visited the city some 26 years later.

A great deal of the property has been long alienated. The main site, with the college and gardens finally became the property of St. Leonard's School for Girls following on several private ownerships.

Before this, one of the buildings of the Old College, the ' Bruce ' building, was used in 1861 for a few brief years by Principal J. D. Forbes in his experiment to revive college residences. Along with the adjoining 17th Century structure it became St. Leonard's Hall, and an elite community formed itself there, including the poet and historian Andrew Lang who subsequently painted many a nostalgic literary picture of his time there.

The chapel was legally excepted from the sale because it was also the parish church. The congregation of St. Leonard's which had worshipped there from the earliest days was removed in 1759, as part of the settlement, to the Collegiate Church of St. Salvator. They continued to worship there separately until 1904 when their own church in Hepburn Gardens, in the west end of the city, was built . . . . well outwith the traditional bounds of the parish. It is distinctive for its Norman-style architecture, and is possibly the last sizeable

130

building to be erected in the ashlar that was traditional of the city's 19th Century buildings.

The ancient chapel lay for generations a shamefully neglected ruin until its skilful restoration by the University in 1952, inspired by the Principal, Sir James Irvine. It was re-dedicated and brought into use in the name of the old college and of the Parish of St. Leonard, whose members still regularly exercise their ancient right of worship there.

That was just a beginning. Irvine had visions of recreating the College of St. Leonard and he paved the way for his dream becoming a reality after his death when the University decided in 1970 to revive their former college.

THE IRONY OF ST. MARY'S

A vast irony surrounds the inception of St. Mary's College which came into existence at a momentous time. Built in 1538 to provide a bulwark of the Catholic faith against the rising tide of heretical Protestantism, the college came within a few years of its completion to be the stoutest religious fortress of the Reformers. It bridged the gap between the two distinct eras of the Medieaval and the Reformed University.

The ' new ' College, as it was first known, was founded for the purpose of equipping men to be sent out to stay the rapid spread of heretical spirit, not only among the laity, but within the University itself. One of the colleges, St. Leonard's, had even openly championed Reform !

But with such irresistible impetus and so overwhelmingly rose the tide of Reformation that St. Mary's, with its Provost, John Douglas, capitulated in 1559 and conformed almost immediately to the new order. Douglas was actually appointed the first Protestant Bishop of St. Andrews at a later date. The Reformers singled out St. Mary's to be their chief school of Protestant teaching in Scotland. In the subsequent fight against episcopacy St. Mary's remained the heart of the anti-Royalist doctrine so long as the Stuart dynasty lasted.

The University, at the time of the Reformation, was modelled on the lines of Oxford and Cambridge, the three residential colleges that comprised it being associated as a complete academic society. It was

131

no longer the only University in Scotland, foundations having been made at Glasgow, Aberdeen and finally at Edinburgh, but it was the most important, having educated almost all the leading figures in national affairs and in the Church.

The college of St. Mary was selected in 1579 by the Reformers for the study of Reformed Theology only, and it has ever since remained a redoubt of the Protestant faith.   How steadfast and enduring that adherence is demonstrated by a series of incidents that occurred four centuries later, as related on p. 153.

The founder of St. Mary's College was the ambitious and ruthless Archbishop James Beaton, uncle of Scotland's first cardinal. He had successfully petitioned the Papacy in 1525 for the erection of a college for the teaching of theology and other disciplines. The project was not authorised until 1538 and St. Mary's was duly instituted, primarily as a college to train candidates for the priesthood. The old Pedagogy was the obvious site and it was duly acquired. The new college buildings were completed by Archbishop Hamilton. The northern and western blocks survive to-day, their ancient austerity mellowed and softened into a lovely precinct corner. They form two sides of a quadrangle which is entered by way of the dignified arched gateway in South Street. A serenely picturesque quadrangle is formed by the surrounding buildings which include the outline of Old Parliament Hall and the much more modern University Library, destined to change its use in the latest university plans. Dominating the centre of the quadrangle stands a spreading Holm Oak of dramatic dimensions.   Although the chapel of St. Mary's has long since disappeared, an aged thorn tree, said to have been planted by Mary, Queen of Scots, leads a propped and precarious existence. In an opposite corner of the quadrangle a shoot from the famous Glastonbury thorn flourishes, planted by a former Principal, G. S. Duncan, a Moderator of the Church of Scotland General Assembly.

The final triumph of Protestanism in 1559 was an event of tremendous and far-reaching consequence in St. Andrews . . . a city that was the very product of the hated Church.   The First Book of Discipline of the Reformers made it reassuringly clear, however, that St. Andrews University would not be abandoned.   Instead, it was chosen to be the principal of the three universities detailed in the Book of Discipline scheme . . . St. Andrews, Aberdeen and Glasgow. St. Andrews was to have three colleges, Arts and Medicine, Law and

Divinity . . . . St. Mary's became the home of the last-named faculty, and in 1579, as stated, was restricted to the study of theology only.

Of the many notable principals of St. Mary's College, Andrew Melville, George Buchanan and Samuel Rutherford, were possibly the most distinguished as scholars and educationists. Melville brought a new life and high academic standards to the university, until his personal intransigence and unyielding opposition to the establishment of episcopacy in Scotland brought about his exile in 1607. A man who could rebuke his King from Holy Trinity pulpit, pluck at his sleeve in public and call him ' God's silly vassal ' was clearly one of no ordinary courage and conviction. This he did in James' own Palace of Falkland where the King had assembled his Church leaders.

Melville was not only one of the most brilliant scholars of his age but he had a genius for organisation, and an unshakable courage.

It was during this period that King James wished to have the university transferred to Perth, under Royal control. The same threat, more forcibly supported, was to be repeated some 150 years later (p. 24).

The next occasion of national strife in which St. Andrews became deeply involved was the Covenanting Movement's violent reaction against episcopal measures. In 1638 the University issued a paper denouncing the Covenant.

But, in a short time both University and Town were persuaded to sign it. Alexander Henderson, a former student of St. Andrews, was Moderator of the historic Glasgow Assembly which effectively demolished the episcopal regime in Scotland. As a consequence, rich revenues of the Archbishopric and the Priory were assigned to the University, although in subsequent Church schisms both Town and Gown lost extensive revenues to the Crown through the machinations of the nation's Regents and their titular appointees, the Tulchan or straw bishops. This was while episcopacy again had assumed a temporary sway.

In the austere days of Covenanting domination the brief restoration era that was to come must have seemed totally inconceivable. Yet, for St. Andrews, the subsequent brutal and autocratic Restoration Government of Charles II brought some brief compensations before the city was finally doomed to lose all ecclesiastical

133

significance, and both city and university sank into a poverty-induced apathy.

For a final fleeting spell only, an exact century after the Reformation, did St. Andrews become prominent. James Sharp, the Reform minister of Crail, became episcopal archbishop of St. Andrews and Chancellor of the University of St. Andrews in 1661. For a time the University entered upon a fruitful existence and exercised a considerable social and political influence. This continued until the final episcopal overthrow when the regime in Scotland vanished for ever.

Decline and decay settled, a black cloud, from the beginning of the 18th Century. A second grave threat to transfer the University to Perth, referred to in another chapter (p. 24) was the most serious of many misfortunes that fell upon the city and on its University alike.

THE LEARNED DOCTOR'S IMPRESSIONS

The torpid state into which St. Andrews had fallen was the subject, more than half a century later, of typically astringent observations by Dr. Samuel Johnson on his 1773 visit. He dined with Principal Murison, and Boswell records the following : ' Dinner was mentioned . . . . '

' Johnson : '' Ay, ay, amidst all these sorrowful scenes I have no objection to dinner.'' '

The ' sorrowful ' scenes referred to acts committed by the Reformers in their attempt to banish all evidences of popery and episcopacy, the results of which had incensed Johnson. In the course of subsequent conversation Boswell asked where John Knox was buried.

Johnson burst out : ' I hope in the highway ' . . ' I have been looking at his reformations.'

Dr. Johnson's visit to the city in 1773 was described both by Boswell and by the lexicographer himself. Boswell confirms the fact that the scholars of St. Andrews were so engrossed in showing the places of academic learning that they allowed the two travellers to leave St. Andrews without even hearing of St. Rule's Tower, let alone seeing it ! Johnson is reported to have kept his head uncovered all the time he spent among the gloomy relics of ecclesiastical vandalism.

134

From College Tower, a corner of St. Salvator buildings, with
the Scores and North Sea beyond.

St. Mary's College, showing the Bell Tower and the propped
Queen Mary's thorn.

(University photograph)

In its remote south-west corner of the University sports field—the Astronomy Department.

He wrote :—

" At an hour somewhat late we came to St. Andrews, a city once archiespiscopal ; where that university still subsists in which philosophy was formerly taught by Buchanan whose name has as fair a claim to immortality as can be conferred by modern latinity, and perhaps a fairer than the instability of vernacular languages admits. We found that by the interposition of some invisible friend lodgings had been provided for us at the house of one of the professors whose easy civility quickly made us forget that we were strangers ; and the whole time of our stay we were gratified by every mode of kindness and entertained with all the elegance of lettered hospitality.

" In the morning we rose to perambulate a city which only history shows to have once flourished, and surveyed the ruins of ancient magnificence of which even the ruins cannot long be visible unless some care be taken to preserve them .... They have been till very lately so much neglected that every man carried away the stones who fancied that he wanted them.

" The cathedral, of which the foundations may be still traced and a small part of the wall is standing, appears to have been a spacious and majestic building, not unsuitable to the primacy of the kingdom. Of the architecture, the poor remains can hardly exhibit even to an artist a sufficient specimen. It was demolished as is well-known, in the tumult and violence of Knox's reformation.

" Not far from the cathedral, on the margin of the water, stands a fragment of the castle in which the archbishop anciently resided. It was never very large and was built with more attention to security than pleasure. Cardinal Beaton is said to have had workmen employed in improving its fortifications at the time when he was murdered by the ruffians of the reformation, in the manner of which Knox has given what he himself calls a merry narrative ....

" The city of St. Andrews, when it had lost its archi-episcopal eminence, gradually decayed ; one of its streets is now lost and in those that remain there is the silence and solitude of inactive indigence and gloomy depopulation.

" The university within a few years consisted of three colleges, but is now reduced to two ; the College of St. Leonard being lately dissolved by sale of its buildings and the appropriation of its revenues to the professors of the two others. The chapel of the alienated college is yet standing, a fabric not inelegant of external structure ;

K

but I was always by some civil excuse hindered from entering it. A decent attempt as I was since told, has been made to convert it into a greenhouse by planting its area with shrubs. This new method of gardening is unsuccessful ; the plants do not hitherto prosper. To what use it will next be put I have no pleasure in conjecturing. It is something that its present state is at least not ostentatiously displayed. Where there is yet shame there may in time be virtue . . . . (The splendid renovation of St. Leonard's Chapel in the middle of the present century justifies the learned doctor's hopes.)

" Of the two colleges yet standing, one is by the institution of its founder appropriated to Divinity. It is said to be capable of containing fifty students, but more than one must occupy a chamber. The library, which is of late erection, is not very spacious, but elegant and luminous. The doctor by whom it was shown hoped to irritate or subdue my English vanity by telling me that we had no such repository of books in England . . . .!

" St. Andrews seems to be a place eminently adapted to study and education, being situated in a populous yet cheap country, and exposing the minds and manners of young men neither to the levity and dissoluteness of a capital city, not to the gross luxury of a town of commerce, places naturally unpropitious to learning . . . . The students, however, are represented as at this time not less than a hundred . . . . .

" Having now seen whatever this ancient city offered to our curiosity we left it with good wishes, having reason to be highly pleased with the attention that was paid to us. But whoever surveys the world must see many things that give him pain. The kindness of the professors did not contribute to abate the uneasy remembrance of a university declining, a college alienated, and a church profaned and hastening to the ground.

" St. Andrews indeed has formerly suffered more atrocious ravages and more extensive destruction, but recent evils affect with greater force . . . . ''

Such were Dr. Johnson's gloomy but accurate impressions.

It was in 1747 that the Crown Commission issued an edict for the union of St. Leonard's and St. Salvator's Colleges into the United College, which marked, incidentally the end until very recently of the ancient St. Andrews teaching system of regents. New buildings at

136

St. Salvator's were completed in 1757 and the St. Leonard's buildings were sold.

Yet St. Andrews, notwithstanding the gloomy and discouraging conditions of which Johnson wrote so acidly, maintained high scholastic standards and a proud academic record among European universities. The colleges also continued to be predominantly residential until the close of the eighteenth century.

TWILIGHT AND A NEW DAWN

So, for more than a century after 1747 the University lived a twilight existence during which it was neglected and seemed to be forgotten completely by the State. Then, in 1826, came its first official visitation in a hundred years, and vast changes followed a searching investigation by the Royal Commission appointed then. The Commissioners authorised the King's Architect for Scotland, Robert Reid, to reconstruct the entire group of university buildings, and particularly the United College. A considerably reformed teaching curriculum was also imposed. Further far-reaching administration changes followed some thirty years later, with the Act of 1858.

Just as in the 20th Century Sir James Irvine was the initiator of a new era as Principal, so was Sir David Brewster, Principal for 20 years until 1859, in the preceding century. He introduced his regime of reform with a notable lack of tact, but with stimulating results. John Tulloch, Principal of St. Mary's College, made that college, at the same time, theologically outstanding once more as it had been two centuries before.

Principal J. D. Forbes who followed Brewster, initiated the first residential scheme on which St. Andrews based its 20th Century expansion. He bought part of the old College of St. Leonard as a student residence, and its success encouraged him to put up a permanent building adjoining. This however did not meet with similar success and was closed in 1874. But the possibilities revealed were obvious. St. Leonard's acquired an ethos. Andrew Lang was its best-known resident student, and its nostalgic influence is imprinted on much of his work.

Crisis for the University came once more in 1876 with a question being asked in Parliament as to its future. The student roll had dropped to 130 ! The University was not then even a potent factor

137

in the city's economy on which it had always exercised a considerable influence.   Given a reprieve, the masters concentrated their energies on trying to increase the student numbers, but with only limited success in the first few years.

A revolutionary step was then taken by the authorities in their attempt to revive their ailing university.   They encouraged women to enrol and in 1883 a fund was inaugurated to provide bursaries for women and to build a hall of residence for them.   This was a *volte-face* indeed.   Only 20 years earlier Elizabeth Garrett, the first woman in Britain to qualify as a doctor of medicine, had been allowed to matriculate at St. Andrews, but her enrolment was subsequently declared illegal by the Senate !   The establishment of University Hall as a residence for women students which subsequently took place in 1892, was in advance of the times as well as a complete change in university policy.   Its wisdom was quickly proven by the enhanced reputation St. Andrews has since acquired as a university for women.

At this time, demands to establish a university, or at least to inaugurate a university college in Dundee attached to St. Andrews, were gaining influential support in that city.   The industrial revolution of the Victorian era and the establishment of a thriving jute trade in which the raw fibre from India was spun and woven in Dundee mills and factories, had tremendously inflated the population and prosperity there.   St. Andrews was merely a village by comparison . . . . a village with a university.   The situation was one that the thriving jute city found increasingly vexatious as its own expansion soared.

The jute fortune of the Baxter family of Dundee was largely responsible for the founding of University College, Dundee, in 1881.   It was a situation, with the smoke-stacked city much larger and of an overwhelmingly greater economic importance than St. Andrews, that could only be a stepping stone.   An insistent cry for full university status in Dundee simply could not be ignored.   The wonder was that the inevitable step took as long as 1967 to achieve finally.

The installation of a Medical School by which St. Andrews was able to grant medical degrees, was one notable result of the union of St. Andrews and Dundee.   The partnership, however, continued uneasily and under constant pressure.   A new building for medicine was erected at the foot of the spacious old garden of St. Mary's College in 1899 through the generosity of Lord Bute, rector of the university, as

138

a stimulus to the medical school which St. Andrews continued to possess until 1972 when its last students were ' capped ' with a St. Andrews degree.

The University entered upon a vital epoch of its history with the end of the First World War. The new era opened with the appointment of James C. Irvine as Principal in 1921. Irvine could well have been making a virtue of necessity when he claimed his ideal was a small elite university. Certainly it was his policy of developing St. Andrews as a residential university that engendered one of the most significant growths in its history. A distinguished chemist, Irvine was also a dynamic administrator. As a first step he revived the system of collegiate residence for men students, and also encouraged the expansion of women's residencies. In this he was immeasurably aided by a donation of £100,000 from Dr. E. S. Harkness, New York. Another notable benefaction was the gift of a new Graduation Hall by Dr. and Mrs Younger of Mount Melville. The Younger Hall in North Street has witnessed many stirring scenes since its completion in 1929.

By the start of the Second World War the student numbers in the university had risen to within sight of 1000, largely due to the residential policy which continued to attract an increasing proportion of women, mostly from south of the border. St. Andrews was still, none the less, the smallest university in Britain with 500 students in the city itself and just under that roll in University College, Dundee. But even during the war, the University, encouraged by Government prompting, was probing into the technological age with an extended field of academic work.

When hostilities ended in 1945 classrooms and laboratories were outdated as well as being crowded with ex-service students of both sexes intent on resuming their interrupted studies. In the next five years enrolments rose to over 2000. But not the least of the post-war problems was to determine the future of the university in Dundee. A Royal Commission in 1953 was followed by an Act that produced a new name for University College, Dundee, which thereafter until 1967 became Queen's College. More important were several changes in the constitution of the university. But this Act only proved an interlude before the final separation of St. Andrews and Dundee in 1967.

Professor T.M., later Sir Malcolm Knox, was appointed Principal in 1953, following the death of Sir James Irvine in the previous year. At the same time the Government accelerated its university education

139

policy with an urgent demand for the provision of more student places all over the country. The number of matriculates at St. Andrews shot up remarkably and exceeded 3000 between St. Andrews and Dundee in 1962/63 session. Extensive developments took place at Queen's College, and with them the pressure increased to separate the two institutions. This was finally brought about in 1967, ironically only a few months before the opening of the Tay Road Bridge, the existence of which could have dissolved many of the physical difficulties that were earlier advanced as the chief reason for separation.

Since then, the Principal, J. Steven Watson, and his fellow administrators, have overcome many of the problems that confronted them by the act of separation, in launching Scotland's oldest university on a new era of expansion.

A UNIVERSITY'S LIBRARY

The separate libraries of the colleges that comprised the University date well before the 16th Century. They combine to make the University Library the oldest in Scotland. But their individual collections were tiny, as the inventories showed when made in 1599.

They include some fine specimens of early printing, dating from 1470, along with many rare volumes and incunabula. The King James VI Library, inaugurated in 1612 by Archbishop Gladstanes who enjoyed the great confidence of James, was not completed until 1643. The building in South Street, together with Parliament Hall beneath it, served generations of students until 1890 when the area was almost doubled with the addition of an Arts Reading Room. Ten years afterwards came a happier extension by Robert Lorimer, the distinguished county architect, to add to the building to the south.

The library, despite its Royal patronage, did not flourish at first. It was due to the Covenanters' Commission of 1641, appointed to reform the University, that it was properly established. In particular, Alexander Henderson, the former St. Andrews student who was the Moderator of the Assembly of the Reformed Church responsible for the Commission, set the Assembly an example by giving £1000 Scots to enable the library to be completed, and so helped in its proper establishment.

Some two years after his gift, the Scottish Parliament met in the hall downstairs, thus giving that building its future name. The meeting took place there because St. Andrews alone of the major Scottish cities had managed to avoid the great plague that swept the nation in 1645. Parliament tried and condemned the supporters of Montrose, captured after the battle at Philiphaugh. Many were executed at the Mercat Cross including members of prominent Scottish families.

The Act of 1707 under which libraries became entitled to a copy of every book published, extended the collection at St. Andrews considerably. In the 18th Century when the libraries of the three colleges were incorporated with that of the University, more space was needed. This was achieved in 1765 and again 65 years later.

Dr. Johnson, on his St. Andrews sojourn, visited the library, but did not manage to see the St. Salvator library, more by design than by accident, it has since been told.

In 1668-74 the distinguished astronomer, James Gregory, conducted many of his astronomical experiments in the Long Room or Upper Gallery, which was restored many years ago to a fitting dignity and beauty and is often used for exhibitions of the library treasures. He employed the sundial in his tests and it rests on a ledge in the Upper Hall. Near the fireplace is Gregory's curious clock, and fixed to a wall outside a window of the Hall the bracket for his telescope is to be seen. Many fine and interesting manuscripts and curios are contained in the cases that line the Hall.

A major problem in an expansion so swift as that of St. Andrews in the present decade is obviously that of library accommodation for its books and for the students to consult them. It had been clear for a considerable time that the existing buildings, filled to their capacity, could no longer suffice. So, after three-and-a-half centuries, the erection of a completely new library building came inevitably to be accepted as an urgent priority.

This building, which will stand in roughly $2\frac{1}{2}$ acres of ground that was part of the old St. Katharine's School for Girls, is planned for the foreseeable future. Its site is strategically placed geographically in relation to the main departments of the University. Its estimated capacity is a book holding of 1,200,000 volumes.

Considerable problems of integration naturally loom large in a historic old town such as St. Andrews. The proposals for the new library are that the block will face east towards the old Arts quadrangle where visitors so delight to linger. It will be linked by a raised way from the quadrangle that will lead to a first-floor level of the library, and will thus relate naturally with the oldest part of the University. To the south of the library block will be the Arts Centre, which will be provided with access ways from North Street. Northwards lies St. Katharine's lawn with its fine trees, and the superb background of St. Andrews Bay. To develop a site at once so important and so central required a great deal of thought and judgment, and it is generally acknowledged that the architect's concept is imaginative and gracious. No doubt its execution will, in the light of previous university buildings, be equally felicitous for St. Andrews as a whole although the plans have been by no means unanimously accepted.

Plans are also well advanced for the new Fine Arts Department of the University to erect an Arts Centre on the southern part of the St. Katharine's site. The Centre is located in St. Katharine's House, a rather fine example of eighteenth century classical architecture which fronts directly on to North Street with an entrance courtyard that is flanked on each side by lodges. This group of buildings forms an essential ingredient of the townscape of St. Andrews and, as such, it is to be preserved. For that reason the new building which will comprise a drama studio/exhibition area, has been designed deliberately to be differential to this classical symmetry and so as not to obtrude on the city's historical character. It will form a wing to St. Katharine's, flanking the entrance court and the present intention is that a future expansion to the Arts Department should form a similar wing on the opposite side of the entrance court. Each area is simple in design, yet is fully equipped with lighting suitable for exhibition and for drama. The highly flexible plans are capable of providing for the needs of artistic and drama societies in the University and also in the town itself—a further Town and Gown extension. A drama workshop will provide the setting for experimentation in student drama and for the production of plays written and produced by students. The whole scheme is also linked with the possibility too of a collection of works of art for the use of the Fine Arts Department and of the University generally.

UNIVERSITY BOTANIC GARDENS

A source of worldwide attraction and an important part of the university is the botanic garden. Although it is situated beside the new Canongate area of the city and well away from any of the

142

The Kennedy mace, presented by the founder of St. Salvator's
in 1461, and fashioned in Paris.

St Salvator's College quadrangle. The east and north wings.

(University photograph).

university's buildings, the garden is a recent location there and it considerably enhances the already attractive appearance of that district. The original botanic garden was formed as long ago as 1889 when beds of plants were laid out by Dr. John Wilson as a teaching aid for his lectures in Botany. The 78 beds contained 828 species of flowering plants and ferns. The site of the first garden was a corner of St. Mary's College grounds covering one-quarter acre, compared to the 20 acres to-day. Additions were regularly made, increasing the area by 1942 to 4½ acres.

As the university acquired more student residences in its twentieth century expansion their grounds have been used to lay down many species of plants. The decision was finally made to move the garden to its new site at the quaintly-named Bassaguard in 1962 . . . . an undulating site bordering the Kinnessburn with a heavy clay soil rich in lime.

The expansive glasshouse range, part of which is open to the public, contains several different environmental units and so enables an infinite variety of plants from most countries of the world to be grown. These potted plants on the glasshouse benches are arranged in families to aid the study of taxonomy. Plants in the corridors are divided into three sections, tropical, sub-tropical and warm-temperate and are arranged in a geographical layout. The collections contain many economic plants of value to students and public alike and are visited by study parties from wide areas to view the wide diversity of form in the plant kingdom. Along with the construction of the glasshouses the surrounding garden was developed. Shelter comprises a mixed coniferous belt of trees to the west which is the prevailing wind direction. Tree and shrub borders are planted across the direction of prevailing winds and produce sheltered places for the cultivation of many wind-tender plants.

Herbaceous and bulbous plants are well established near the glasshouse range for teaching purposes and to give a long and lasting display of flowers throughout spring and summer. Order beds similar to those planted by Wilson in 1899 have been established and these have been laid out according to the evolutionary taxonomic principles of Cronquist and Takhtajan in a layout quite different from the straight lines of the rectangular beds of earlier design. Here will be found some 141 beds, each containing the hardy species of plants.

The rock garden and scree contain alpine plants from all five continents and it is interesting to be able to observe species from

L

South Africa and Australia flowering side by side with those of South America and the Himalayas.

A limestone section in the rock garden contains predominantly British species and is constructed to show the rocky outcrops of limestone which is evident in the mountains and also the limestone pavement formation which is a feature of the Burren in West Ireland. Indeed, many plants which occur at the Burren flourish here.

Close by, an extensive area has been constructed to ensure that the acid-loving plants can be grown, as, while the natural soil has a high lime content and is heavy clay in texture, peat has been incorporated in quantity to provide this lime-free area. Many genera are grown here without difficulty, with rhododendron, pieris, vaccinium, primula and gentian predominating.

A heath garden contains a wide variety arranged so that at any time of the year flowers can be seen. Of horticultural merit are the many forms of colour foliage now available among the heaths, (Erica) and heathers (Calluna). Other plants such as dwarf conifers, ferns and rhododendrons have been added to give a contrasting foliage effect and to lend the area a sense of scale.

Conifers play a large part in the garden's life, not only as shelter trees and foliage effect, but also as specimen plants and for teaching purposes. A pinetum has been established comprising the hardiest specimen of forest tree together with their dwarf mutants in such a manner as to display the variety of forms and size easily.

A research area of $3\frac{1}{2}$ acres is set aside from the public for use by the Department of Botany for its experimental work in genetics, taxonomy and physiology.

The solitary portion of the former botanic garden retained is at Dyers Brae, south of St. Mary's College. It provides a unique microclimate where sub-tropical plants can be grown on the wall terraces and where many plants which would not survive at Bassaguard grow well, thanks to the climatic effect, coupled with better soil conditions.

The botanic garden is open to the public Monday to Friday from 10 a.m. to 4 p.m. and the glasshouses in the afternoons from 2-4 p.m. Entry to them is gained from the Canongate.

144

TOWN AND GOWN RELATIONS

Viewing the vast complex of new buildings—vast in relation to the area of the city itself—required to contain an expanding population of some three thousand students to-day makes it difficult to grasp the fact that a century ago the university was a tiny and impoverished institution with an enrolment of 130, its very existence in jeopardy.

In reaching present dimensions its buildings now occupy about a third of the city's available acreage. The remaining land is the living space of some 10,500 inhabitants who are ' non-university '.

It is doubtful if any other community exists where a university plays so dominant a role in the local economy. The relevance of recent and contemplated expansion of the Gown on this scale to the prosperity of the Town is obvious.

The situation also poses naturally the question of relations between Town and Gown. In the post-war years that relationship has been amicable at best, and at worst, mutually tolerant. This says a great deal for both sides in view of the expanse of generation gap that divides them. St. Andrews, the town, consists of a community of older, retired people ; the University effervesces with exuberant youth. Situations of strain have occasionally arisen, as they must, but that such situations have been few and relatively unimportant is highly creditable to both. The citizens do not regard an increase in student population to an ultimate 4000 with misgiving.

A new factor in Town and Gown relations has recently emerged. This was the lowering of the voting age to 18 years, presenting a powerful bloc of students with the ability to influence municipal as well as parliamentary elections. In St. Andrews the balance of student population, plus the traditional apathy of local electors, can well decide any purely local issue or candidature. Under Regionalisation the students can continue to have considerable say in the election of Regional and District councillors.

Incidentally, one student will go down in the history of this period as holder of a unique double record. Robert B. Jones will have been the first, and the last student-member of the St. Andrews Town Council, prior to being superseded by the North Fife District that forms part of the projected Tayside Region.

The relationship between these disparate groups is one that has revealed itself as fraught with explosive incidents in universities everywhere ; much more so in recent years when the student body has become a not inconsiderable political force and something of a social problem.

St. Andrews has lived with the situation for centuries, and both communities have handled it well, on the whole, not always an easy task, as history shows.

Indeed, the first recorded case of Town and Gown friction came only thirty years after the University's foundation. Bishop Kennedy, one of the University's greatest figures, intervened in 1444 in a dispute with the citizens over the jurisdiction of the Rector. R. G. Cant, in his ' University of St. Andrews ' writes :—'' Kennedy's solution was a most tactful adjustment of the rights of the university and the civic pride of the city.'' Subsequent incidents were not handled always so diplomatically.

Privileges that were granted to the University on its founding were a constant bone of contention with the citizens for some centuries. A notable occasion was the bitter confrontation that led to the threat by the masters in 1697 to remove the University to Perth, some thirty miles distant. The story of that incident is told on p. 24.

Generally the atmosphere between the two bodies has been one of mutual tolerance, with occasional animosity distilled with some intervals of warm appreciation and close co-operation. Such a time was the quincentenary celebrations in 1911 of the University's founding. The scale of the ceremonies demanded and received a joint effort that reflected fittingly the prestige of both Town and Gown communities.

The Town Hall and other civic buildings were made available for the accommodation of the hundreds of academic dignitaries who descended on St. Andrews from almost every centre of learning over the world. Garden parties, banquets and receptions were held, both university and civic. The quincentenary ceremony itself was distinguished by a memorable display of oratory from the Rector, Lord Rosebery. It was the last, and possibly, the most lavish old-style ' great occasion ' in St. Andrews before World War One ushered in a new, less opulent and less colourful era.

An earlier date that stands out dramatically at the other extreme in the history of Town and Gown relations saw the support of the Town ranged solidly behind the students against their masters. This was March, 1881, when the students' Kate Kennedy procession was banned by Principal J. C. Shairp and went into limbo for 45 years. The history of the ' Kate Kennedy ' is believed to go back to the 15th Century. A festival of a kind similar to the 19th Century annual procession which dated back to the 1840s was condemned in the early days by the University authorities. By the late 19th Century years the revived procession had again degenerated into a drunken rabble.

It emerged once more in 1926 in a form completely different from that of its origins, as a dignified pageant that nowadays is pleasurably acceptable to the University hierarchy and to the townspeople.

That was far from being the case in 1881. The ' Kate Kennedy ' was a thorn in the flesh to Principal Shairp and to many of his colleagues. The incident that led to its banning was a series of lampoons which in previous years had greatly infuriated the authorities, particularly the Principal, their chief target.

On the day in March that the students assembled outside the Cross Keys Hotel in Market Street for their annual revel a blizzard was sweeping the city. Huge, white-capped rollers were mounting in the bay.

A day of long-remembered drama was beginning.

In the midst of the revelry Principal Shairp passed by. An incident, never fully clarified, occurred, It resulted in the Principal informing the police. The charge subsequently levelled against the students could not be explained away by student high spirits. A court case against a number of them was the sequel. It failed, but in spite of that, or may be because of it, twenty students were rusticated

The Principal's splenetic vengeance was followed by a public meeting in the Town Hall where the townspeople, who enjoyed the annual celebration, enthusiastically passed resolutions in favour of the students.

But the ' Kate Kennedy ' was foreshortened that final year, not by the Principal's spleen, but by a nearby tragedy. The celebration came to a sudden end for ever in that particular form.

The noisy procession of roystering students had just entered South Street when the Kirk Hill's cannon boom announced that a ship was in distress in the bay. Both Town and Gown forgot Kate Kennedy and all rushed to the shore. Two ships were seen through the blizzard to be in dire straits, with a ferocious gale pounding them on to the jagged rocks near the harbour.

Both foundered in the storm that raged all day. One, the
"Harmonie" was wrecked in the morning, and the other, the
"Merlin" met its doom by the afternoon, with the loss of five lives.
Gaily-costumed students rushed to the beach to help in the rescues.
Many souvenirs still exist in the town of that tragic day in the shape
of articles rescued from the vessels when the broken pieces of wreck-
age were washed up on the beaches.

In the following year, 1882, the students were prepared to defy
the Principal and carry on with their procession. First, they were
refused to hold a ball in the College Hall, and then the order went
out they dare not ignore.

> "That, rather than Kate's Bell should toll,
> They'd rusticate and close the whole."

SIGNIFICANCE OF KATE KENNEDY

" If you had been ;
You would have been born in Spring "

(Kate's Bard, 1970)

FORTY-FIVE years passed before the celebrations were held again. Since the revival of the " Kate Kennedy " as a historical pageant in 1926 the procession has enjoyed a deserved popularity with Town, Gown and holidaymakers. The Club is the jealously guarded preserve of male students, which was one of the two conditions laid down when it was resumed, thanks to the active co-operation of Principal J. C. Irvine. The other condition was that the " K. K. Annual ", published on the day of the pageant, " should eschew scurrilities."

Both conditions have been faithfully observed and so cemented a bright future for the pageant. A relaxation has been the permission to women students to take part in the procession as suitable female characters.

The Kate Kennedy Club has since been carried on by third-year and older students in a manner highly commendable for its dignity and traditional ceremony. Irvine's purpose in allowing its revival has been admirably fulfilled, to the benefit of Town and Gown. Briefly that is : " to keep green the memory of the niece of Bishop Kennedy, and to instil an appreciation of the historical basis of St. Andrews whose past inspires in most students an enduring love for the city."

A ' beardless bejant ' or first-year student, represents the legendary ' Kate '. Seated in a flower-decked carriage, ' she ' is accompanied by the venerable Bishop Kennedy, her uncle, and attended by pages and knights in mediaeval costume. In the procession march or ride men whose deeds have fashioned the history of the university and of the city from earliest days. The parade leaves the ancient quadrangle of St. Salvator's College to the solemn peal of Kate's Bell. Symbolically in the lead strides St. Andrew, barefoot and bearing his cross before him. The event includes ceremonial calls on the Provost and Magistrates of the city, and the Principals of the University and St. Mary's College who all pay homage and present gifts to the Lady Kate. Nowadays the celebration takes place in the less rigorous weather of April rather than the very early days of Spring as was formerly the custom. The characters portrayed conduct the spectator through the history of Town and Gown. St. Andrews University has had no lack in its existence of approaching six centuries of outstanding figures . . . . soldiers, courtiers, scientists, poets and romantics. The early courtier-poets include William Dunbar, Sir Robert Aytoun, Gavin Douglas and Sir David Lindsay of the Mount ; poets of the past century are represented by Andrew Lang and R. F. Murray ; contemporary with Burns was his fervent admirer, Robert Fergusson of tragic genius. Among the soldiers are numbered Montrose and Argyle. The charisma of Montrose clings to a surprising degree in Scotland to-day, while the romantics include the prodigious Admirable Crichton, ' graduate at 14 years of age, of wonderful intellectual gifts, combined with remarkable prowess in swordmanship and all the knightly graces '. Another rommantic figure was John Honey, the student of divinity who in 1800 seven times swam out to a wreck in the East Bay, each time returning with a rescued sailor. The strain and effort brought him to an early grave. He was rewarded by the city with a testimonial of thanks !

Appropriate recent additions to the ghostly parade are Irvine himself, and D'Arcy Thompson, the remarkable and beloved scientist who became a professor at 24 and held a Chair for more than sixty years. D'Arcy Thompson travelled the world in his eighties, a tall striking and vigorous man, brief of speech and to the point. On one occasion leaving the local train from St. Andrews at Leuchars, five miles distant, he remarked to a colleague :—" Well, that's the worst part of the journey over."

" Oh," said his companion, " Are you off to Dundee ?"

" No, Delhi !" was the terse reply.

Few St. Andrews men have achieved more in world history than the local farmer's son, James Wilson, whose birthplace would be a shrine for American tourists . . . . if it were known ! Many patriotic Americans have sought it out.

More than any other man Wilson shaped the Constitution of the United States following the War of Independence. Associate of Benjamin Franklin, the first American to be honoured by St. Andrews with the freedom of the city, and of George Washington, Wilson was

(*University photograph*).

Centrepiece of the K. K. pageant : the coach bearing the Lady Katharine and her uncle, Bishop Kennedy.

Students at the Department of Physical Sciences in the North Haugh precinct.

Modern architecture of Andrew Melville Hall at the North Haugh.

not honoured until 108 years after his death by his adopted country when his ashes were removed from an obscure grave in North Carolina to lie beside his old associate, Franklin, in Philadelphia.

It was this graduate of St. Andrews University who first propounded the idea of the United States to be considered as " one undivided, independent nation ".

Wilson it was who did more to draft the adopted constitution of the United States, than any other man.   He was the first and unpopular advocate of the democratic view of one single executive head of the state . . . . a President, to be elected by the people directly as President of the United States.

Yet he is a prophet with little honour in the land of his birth.

This remarkable St. Andrean matriculated in the United College at the age of 15 years.   He arrived in America in the midst of the first colonial fury over the Stamp Act and in a few years became the first holder of the Chair of English Literature in the College of Philadelphia.   He turned to Law and became deeply involved in American politics.   As a congressman for Pennsylvania, he helped signally by his views and his oratory in the adoption of the American Constitution by the majority of the separate States.   Washington made him one of the first Justices of the Supreme Court and Wilson set his signature to the historic Declaration of Independence.

Many visiting Americans express deep disappointment that St. Andrews can offer no link with one of the outstandingly great men of American history—the son of a district farmer whose birthplace, in the vicinity the records have failed to reveal.   Only his place in the ghostly parade of the ' Kate Kennedy ' recalls the man who played a leading part in founding the United States of America.

THE PLACE OF THE RECTOR

The triennial rectorial election is primarily another student occasion that celebrates perpetuation of one of the oldest offices in the university's hierarchy.

The Rector of the University, in its earliest days, was a figure of considerable power and dignity.   In rank he came next to the Chancellor himself.

Following the considerable changes effected in the administrative structure of the University by the Reformed Church, the Rector was

M   151 given even greater powers over the colleges. As example, when James VI and I visited the city in 1607 it was the Rector who received him as representative of the University.

Further radical changes in administration came as the result of the Royal Commission in 1826. A searching inquiry into the affairs of the University resulted in a drastic diminution of the Rector's authority. The Act of 1858 carried this curtailment much further by reducing the office of rector to something of a formality. He became a representative of the students, his duty being to speak for them on the University Court.

The professors and graduates were accordingly not permitted to take part in his election which fell entirely on the student body. It was in this way that, from 1858, the present rectorial ceremonial gradually arose. The students generally chose a distinguished figure in public life, one whose own fame would add prestige to the appointment. He would deliver his address to the students, but would leave the affairs of the Court to its members. A long line of rectors distinguished in a wide range of fields has since duly represented the students. In the present century they have included Lord Rosebery in 1911 when the quincentenary celebrations were held, Kipling, Nansen, the explorer, J. M. Barrie whose address on ' Courage ' became famous, Andrew Carnegie, and so on. In the opinion of many, the appointment of T.V. personality, John Cleese in 1970 as Rector, represented an unfortunate departure from tradition, but during his term of office Mr Cleese proved a potent force on the University Court and admirably maintained its dignity.

The traditional ceremony surrounding the Rector's installation is a picturesque and rather delightful part of the University scene in St. Andrews ; a good-humoured occasion that is handled with commendable restraint. The students gather at the West Port to greet their elected representative and welcome him with a scholarly address in Latin delivered by the President of the Students' Representative Council. The Rector is ushered into a horse-drawn coach which, for the occasion is dragged by a team of husky athletic ' blues ' on a round of visitations throughout the town. This has expanded to include several of the new residences, and soon the rectorial carriage is laden with gifts from his student constituents, many of them bizarre and distinctly risible.

At intervals, the triumphal passage, headed by an enthusiastic band of kilted pipers, is interrupted to receive the homage of a variety of student organisations. In the course of the route, the Rector is offered the respects of the Provost and Magistrates of the city, as well as hospitality from the Principal of St. Mary's College. His final destination is the residence of the Principal of the University where he is an honoured guest.

The evening becomes a round of student revelling which includes a torchlight procession to the sea front where a bonfire and fireworks are traditional parts of the celebrations.

THE LONG MEMORY

An acute awareness of history and tradition is an integral part of St. Andrews. It lingers never far beneath the placid surface of every stratum of local life. In modern times this has occasionally evinced itself within the inner circles of the university in an undeclared attitude towards Roman Catholicism.

This attitude was moulded over 400 years ago in the fires of post-Reformation struggles when St. Mary's, founded as a Catholic College, became the stronghold of Protestant Church of Scotland teaching.

True, Cardinal Gordon Gray, a highly distinguished graduate of St. Andrews, had bestowed on him in 1967 an honorary Doctorate of Divinity by his *alma mater*. As Archbishop Gray, he created history when he was invited, and accepted, to preach in the University Church of St. Salvator, the first Roman Catholic to do so for over 400 years. He was later elected honorary president of the University Theological Society, a body established in 1764. This involved delivering a presidential address in the university in 1972.

On the other hand, Sir John Rothenstein, elected by the students as their Rector (1964-67) afterwards complained in his memoirs, of scarcely concealed hostility towards himself during his first two years in office. He also referred to ' a degree of religious bigotry in some senior sections of the university that he was unaware still existed anywhere in the world.'

An earlier distinguished Roman Catholic, the Marquis of Bute, who was elected Rector in 1892, aimed at using his influence in that office to restore St. Andrews University to what he believed to be its ancient form of a ' complete university '. Part of this plan involved associating his Church with the work of St. Andrews by settling

153

Blair's College in the Priory as an affiliated college of the university. Lord Bute did much good work for the University and gave substantial donations to its funds, but in this plan he did not succeed.

Perhaps most indicative of this ambivalence that combined a readiness to co-operate in some degree of ecumenism with an unexpressed determination to keep the Roman Catholic hierarchy in Scotland out of St. Andrews, was an incident in 1948.

At that time the massively jarring, red sandstone pile of the Grand Hotel that looms conspicuously over the Tom Morris Green of the Old Course, became a storm-centre of violent controversy. This quickly revealed fierce religious overtones. Information became public that the Catholic Church was interested in buying the hotel, with the intent of establishing itself once more in the city that four centuries earlier had been the capital of Catholicism in Scotland. The proposal was to set up a theological college. Undercurrents stirred and rippled ominously. They quickly rose to a boiling maelstrom.

A public protest meeting was called, at which a professor of St. Mary's Divinity College was the sole speaker. He made the public statement that it was the policy of the Roman Catholic Church to make St. Andrews the centre for Roman Catholic propaganda and for a conversion of Scotland ! A committee, chaired by another Church of Scotland minister, presented a petition to the city's authorities demanding that they use their planning powers to stop the sale. The upshot was that the shareholders of the Hotel Company changed their minds and refused the Catholic Church offer.

Some weeks later the Hotel was bought . . . . by the University authorities ! They converted it first into a residence for male students, and to-day it houses a community of girl students, as Hamilton Hall ; named, let it be hastened to add, after the present Chancellor of the University, the Duke of Hamilton, and not one of the Protestant martyrs.

By contrast to this seemingly encrusted hierarchical policy of the University, the present-day attitude of Town and Gown in general towards religion is far removed from the bigotries of four centuries ago. It could be fairly said that the several denominations represented at this time display a lethargic amity, one towards the other, that passes as liberal and ecumenical.

154

ACADEMIC CIRCUMSTANCE

The occasionally grey atmosphere of the city is still at times brightened as a consequence of the ritual associated with academic occasions. Colourful scholastic gowns and hoods worn by the teaching staffs are produced at graduations and formal processions and gatherings. The complete system of this formal wear was modelled as recently as 1867 on the ancient academic costume of Paris university. It was there that many Scotsmen were educated in the far-off days before their country possessed a university of its own. The academic hoods were added in the pattern of Cambridge.

A prominent place in this traditional ritual is occupied by the magnificent symbolic maces carried before the Principal and his Senate. The maces are six in number, three of them of fifteenth century fashioning, which have been in almost continuous use, and three which have been added during the present century. The ancient maces are those of the Faculty of Arts, the Faculty of Canon Law and the College of St. Salvator. The mace presented to University College, Dundee, was wrought in 1912, one for the School of Medicine was presented in 1949. The third, secured for the university as distinct from its constituent faculties, was made in 1958, the head taking the form of a figure of St. Andrew (p. 149).

Other university treasures are an opulent collection of college plate used for ceremonial occasions, including two mazers, or grace cups, and various silver cups, and archery medals.

An archery competition for the Silver Arrow was a feature of university life in the 1600's and 1700's. It was open to all students of the university and normally took place at the Bow Butts overlooking the Links. Past winners were the Royalist Montrose, and Argyle, his implacable enemy. The last competition was held in 1754, coincidentally the year of the Royal and Ancient Golf Club's founding. Golf had taken over from toxophily ! (p. 66).

The familiar scarlet gown worn by the St. Andrews students has a severely practical purpose. The original garment was a skimpy affair that reached down only to the knee and its thin material provided no protection against the cold of a St. Andrews winter and spring. In 1838 successful petition was made for something more practical. The gown was re-designed to serve as a cloak and was made in warm-looking and warmth-giving scarlet flannel.

Over the 19th Century years one or two traditions that are reminders of the more spartan days of their hardy predecessors were
born and still persist. Meal Monday holiday recalls the days when
many of the students, sons of the Scottish manse and of farms and
even tiny crofts, walked miles over mountains and glens to the university, carrying as part of their baggage strapped to their shoulders,
enough oatmeal to last them half the academic session. They were
allowed a long week-end respite from studies at mid-term to return
home for replenishment of their staple food supplies.

With its time-honoured demand of a pound of raisins in return
for a ' receipt ', invariably ribald in character, Raisin Monday is a
survival of the initiation into university life of first-year students, or
bejants (*bec jaune*, or yellow beaks) as they are known at St. Andrews.

Recently, an ancient general holiday has been restored to Town
and Gown both. The celebration of St. Andrew's Day on November
30th was, for centuries, one of the principal holy days in the city. It
fell into disfavour following the sweeping changes in the wake of
Reformation.

The students, with a seemingly deeper regard for history than the
townspeople, took the lead in campaigning persistently before succeeding in persuading the university authorities to restore the traditional holiday. The Town has since followed suit. Once more it is
celebrated as a general holiday to commemorate the founder saint of
St. Andrews. To-day through the martyr saint, the holiday brings
annual reminder of the city's former ecclesiastical eminence, and of
St. Andrew's affinity with home and exiled Scots.

A warm bond of attachment to their *alma mater* has been a constant St. Andrews evocation down the years. Numerous traditions
and customs perpetuated by succeeding generations of matriculates
provide one proof of that bond.

Nostalgia is a recurring theme in the writings of mature former
students, well typified in the verse of R. F. Murray, the American-
St. Andrews poet :—

" Life has not since been wholly vain ;
And now I bear of wisdom plucked from joy and pain
Some slender share.
But, however rich the store, I'd lay it down
To feel upon my back once more,
The old red gown."

LEUCHARS

THE OLD AND THE NEW

SIX miles to the north-west of St. Andrews the village of Leuchars, its nuances a pitfall to unfamiliar Sassenach tongues, is worthy of more than a passing visit.   The area is unusual in that it is untypical of Scotland as a whole.   The name (anglicè Loo-kars) derives from the village hinterland of low-lying ground, once a morass that surrounded the village from west by the north to east.   Centuries ago this wide area lay under water for the greater part of each year, and was Scotland's nearest approach to fenland.   Flat-bottommed boat was then the most usual form of transport.

The area now known as Tentsmuir, has known several civilisations, including an early Danish invasion and settlement.   It is rich in pre-historic relics including a chalice credited to 2000 B.C. Tentsmuir Point Nature Reserve, as well as being a migratory resting place, is a huge winter roost for wildfowl of all kinds.   Access by car is just possible to the solitary foreshore of Kinshaldy Beach.   The artificial Morton Lochs two miles north of Kinshaldy are also on the migration route and a haven for wildfowl and waders.   There is a well-constructed hide in the Morton nature reserve.

The village of Leuchars itself is to-day associated with the newest as well as the oldest in Britain.   Part of its original marshland has become a key base in the nation's aerial defence.

Within 200 yards of airfield runways where Britain's newest service aircraft take off, and vying in antiquity with the oldest building in St. Andrews, is the distinctive Parish Church of St. Athernase.   In a bull of Pope Gregory IV, dated 1187, reference is made to the church of Lochres, and the Norman architecture was completed by Roger di Quincy who, like his father, Seier di Quincy, was a crusader in the early twelfth century.   The church was dedicated in 1244 by Bishop de Bernheim, and by him placed under the guardianship of St. Athernase.   It is therefore upwards of 700 years old.   The bell tower surmounting the vaulting of the apse, is a late seventeenth century embellishment, but has been mellowed by time into a harmonious addition to the main structure.　The apse and chancel are considered to be the second finest fragment in Britain of Norman architecture.

The most notable minister of the ancient church was Alexander Henderson who became Moderator of the momentous Glasgow Assembly of 1638 and was a leading figure in the drafting of the Solemn League and Covenant.　He was variously described as the most able of the men present at that momentous gathering and as ' a moderator without moderation ' when the Assembly abolished episcopacy in Scotland.　Yet, years after he left his church of Leuchars the General Assembly of 1649 ordered the removal of the magnificent chancel screen from the church as being too reminiscent of episcopalian frippery !　Henderson, as we have already noted, did set his Assembly an example when he donated money to the first University Library of St. Andrews—a notable and inspiring gift.

Born of the Crusades, St. Athernase has witnessed the ascendancy of the Mediaeval Church ; it passed safely through the stirring times of the Reformation ;　it was in the very centre of the struggle between Episcopacy and Presbyterianism, and at the Revolution Settlement in 1688 it became the home of a simple Presbyterian worship.　Now, over seven centuries on, it stands, a venerable landmark and an inspiration to all who value history and tradition.

After the death of Roger di Quincy, the castle and barony of Leuchars passed into the hands of the Comyns, a family destined to play an important part in the history of Scotland.　John Comyn, having been involved in the treason of the Red Comyn in the stirring times of Robert the Bruce, his Barony of Leuchars was forfeited and the estate was divided into three sections.　The old Castle of Leuchars was demolished in the early 1800's.

Captain Andrew Bruce of Earlshall, which was one of the three divisions of the estate, built the mansion of that name.　It dates back to 1546.　He earned the hatred of the Covenanters through his zeal as a soldier against them.　He heavily defeated Hackston of Rathillet, and other Cameronians at Airdsmoss.　Hackston, as we related, was taken prisoner and suffered death in the Grassmarket for his share in the murder of Archbishop Sharp (p. 19).　Earlshall was uninhabited for 70 years after 1822 and it was restored by Sir Robert Lorimer, the noted architect, who did so much valuable restoration work in Fife around the turn of the century.　The old fireplace in the principal hall has a lintel formed of a huge monolith that bears the

Part of the North Haugh precinct. Madras College sports field in the foreground.

(University photograph).

Part of the Order Bed layout of plants at the University Botanic Garden in Canongate.

(University photograph).

arms and initials of the founder of the mansion, Andrew Bruce, and his wife, Elizabeth Leslie.

Pitlethie House, in the immediate vicinity of Earlshall, is said to have been a Royal hunting seat frequented by James III, James IV, Mary Queen of Scots, and James VI, and it is quite probable also that some if not all of these monarchs worshipped in the venerable Kirk of Leuchars.

The twentieth century science of aeronautics brought a measure of prosperity to the ancient and sleepy village, almost immediately after the authorities had discovered the importance of the surrounding flat lands in flying.

It was in 1911 that the army, through the Royal Engineers started experimenting with balloons in the area, but the development of the airfield proper did not begin until some time during the First World War. The Royal Navy first saw its possibilities for flying machines and they started a Fleet Training School at Leuchars. The Station became part of the Royal Flying Corps. Then the Royal Air Force as the service became known, took it over in 1920, continuing its flying training role until 1938. It then became a full operational base of Coastal Command.

Leuchars remained under that Command throughout the Second World War. It supported not only Royal Air Force squadrons, but also units from Australia, Norway and the Netherlands, and from New Zealand. Their duties involved every form of maritime operation and reconnaisance. The famous Mosquito incursions into Europe mapped the prelude of the shattering bombing raids to come.

In 1950 the Station was again transferred, this time to Fighter Command. Since then it has been the home of many famous R.A.F. squadrons flying every type of jet fighter. Leuchars became one of the few fighter bases remaining in the United Kingdom and continued in that capacity when its parent Command became absorbed by the Strike Command formed in 1968. It is equipped with the latest British aircraft. The air station makes Leuchars, where the Queen, Prince Philip and other members of the Royal family have frequently visited, almost as well known as St. Andrews itself.

THE EAST NEUK OF FIFE

CRAIL

ST. ANDREWS lies on a part of the Fife coastline that looks northwards to the hills of Angus and the Cairngorms mountain beyond. To the south of the historic little city runs a high ridge that provides to the north a glorious panorama of the rugged northern landscape, south-ward it looks over the wide waters of the Forth into East Lothian.

Eastwards that ridge descends gently to the sea at Fife Ness That point marks the outermost edge of the Firth of Forth estuary. The coastline from there turns west and south and its first few miles of cliffs and sands are occupied by a group of the most interesting and historic fishing villages in Scotland.

They are the townships of the East Neuk of Fife. ' Neuk ', of course, is the old Scots word for corner, and right in the very corner is the first of these villages, Crail, whose name ' Car-ail ' simply says in a literal translation, ' corner town '. Some historians, however, aver that the meaning is ' Royal Town '. Actually both interpreta-tions are apt.

In all its lengthy history, Crail has lived within the orbit of the St. Andrews sphere of influence, some ten miles distant, first as an ecclesiastical suburb, and latterly as a holiday resort with many indi-vidual features to commend it. The ancient fishing village and med-iaeval trading port followed the example of its larger neighbour by introducing an era of cautious modernisation a century ago, after 200 years of little change. Its streets to-day are lined with many of the red pantiled houses so typical of Fife of the eighteenth century, eman-ating the old-world charm of that period. Indeed, the lovely old township preserves a timeless air and it bountifully repays exploration of a plethora of beauty spots and historic buildings. Crail is the oldest of the five Neuk villages. The others are strung, jewels in a sparkling necklace, along the northern edge of the Forth's estuary ... a breathtaking coastline. They are Anstruther, Pittenweem, St. Monance and Elie.

The harbour of the burgh is as old as Crail itself and its steep and winding streets leading up to the broad Marketgate have been trodden down the ages by seafarers from many parts of the continent. It possesses an interesting seventeenth century customs house which indicates the extent of the trade that had for long been carried on with the Low Countries. As long ago as 1575 Crail and Pittenweem ranked equally in eleventh place for volume of trade and importance in Scotland. They were among the chief gateways for the Scots to the wealth and the learning of Europe.

For centuries until some fifty years ago the North Sea herring shoals were the backbone of the Neuk's staple industry of fishing, but a major mystery of ecology was the sudden and dramatic departure of the herring from that sea area. There has been no subsequent sign of the shoals ever returning. Nowadays shellfish, particularly lobsters, along with white fish, form the main catches netted by the line and seine net fishermen on their oft-dangerous outings.

But the days when innumerable sea superstitions coloured the lives of the fisherfolk have died out in Crail. Skate brew, or soup, is rarely mentioned nowadays, for instance, as a sovereign remedy for a childless marriage. Such superstitions, together with the old customs, do linger to some extent in the other, more closely-knit fishing villages which have not experienced the same infusion of prosperous incomers that Crail has attracted.

The burgh's story goes back into pre-history, and relics of the Bronze Age are on exhibit to testify to its great age. A number of cliff caves have associations with early man, and, like St. Andrews, it possesses its legendary Blue Stane. This is situated at the entrance to Crail Church, formerly Old St. Mary's. The site has been occupied by a church since the twelfth century, making it one of the most ancient religious places in Scotland. The existing fabric has been restored and repaired at intervals down the centuries. The churchyard contains interesting old tombstones and also a mort house that was used to thwart the notorious bodysnatchers of the early 1800s. Crail suffered severely from these ghoulish ravages. The inscription on the mort house, situated in a corner of the churchyard, reads :— "Erected for securing the dead—1826".

One of the burgh's archaelogical treasures is a Pictish slab believed to belong to the Eighth Century.

Constantine's Cave, often called 'The Devil's Cove' is associated with that unfortunate Scottish King who lost his life battling against Danish invaders around 874. For some two centuries the

162

Danes harried the Fife coastline, although there must have been some peaceful settlement for it was at Crail they learned the culinary art of curing herring. Dane's Dyke is believed to have been erected by them and they also settled at Tentsmuir, north of St. Andrews.

The Caiplie Caves have the name of having provided habitation for the Columban missionaries, who peacefully invaded Fife and founded the Culdee Church. They included St. Adrian, the Burgh's patron saint, who died at the hands of the Danes.

David I, who so consistently favoured the establishment of the Roman Church, often resided at Crail Castle, and the north barns of Crail came to be known as the Kings barns, perpetuated in the nearby village of that name. But it was Robert the Bruce, Scotland's hero, who granted Crail its first burgh charter. One of the markets this authorised was held on Sundays. Long after the Reformation in Scotland in which Crail was destined to play so significant a part, the villagers stubbornly held to their traditional right of Sunday for the market, even after the stern Reformers had legally altered the market day to Saturday. It was not until half a century later that the compromise of Friday as market day was reached. The present Market Cross, with its conspicuous unicorn atop, is not old, although the pediment is a respected sixteenth century. It stands on the site of earlier crosses which marked the granting and perpetuation of the market.

Also, as with St. Andrews, Crail conducted a Flemish and Dutch trade in mediaeval times. A Dutch bell tower, with its bell cast in Holland, dated 1520, still adorns the old Town Hall. The tolling of curfew each night at ten o'clock except Sundays is a still continued custom.

In addition to royalty, noted ecclesiastics were associated with the village, including the Melvilles, both uncle and nephew. A later minister of the church was James Sharp, afterwards to become Episcopal Bishop of St. Andrews until his assassination by the Covenanters (p. 19).

Crail knew well the magnetic personality of preacher John Knox. It was from its church of St. Mary and then in St. Andrews that he preached his famous inflammatory sermon that sparked off the Reformation.

To turn to a subject far removed from religion, although possibly not so far removed in the eyes of some of its devotees, Crail is the birthplace of the seventh oldest golf club in the world. Its Golfing

Society was formed in 1786 when the linkslands which are overlooked by the old castle, were formally transformed without much effort into the sporting Balcomie Golf Course, pleasantly cliff-girt and beach-bounded.

*　　*　　*　　*　　*　　*　　*　　*　　*

The Island of May, six miles offshore from Crail, is to-day best known as a bird sanctuary of considerable importance to ornothologists, particularly in the study of migratory birds in which notable research has been carried out since 1907 at the island. It is the most easterly of the several islands in the Firth of Forth and the last landfall for many birds of passage on their way south. It has a long history and like many other islands on Scotland's eastern seaboard, was a haven for early Christian evangelists. Of these St. Adrian is commemorated in several of the East Neuk villages and he was, in fact, killed on May Island by one of the innumerable raiding Danish marauders, circa 870. After the re-establishment of the Scottish kingdom by Robert the Bruce following Bannockburn the island was assumed into the St. Andrews bishopric. The remains of the thirteenth century chapel dedicated to St. Adrian, still to be seen on the island, are important. Its monks maintained their priory for two centuries, constantly faced with Norse raids, which finally compelled them to settle in Pittenweem.

Commanding the entrance to the Firth of Forth on its northern coast, the island's strategic position meant that it played roles of varying importance in the wars between Scotland and England as well as against pirates. Although it is an important lighthouse base, it is also a nature reserve possessed of better than average soil for a small island and therefore able to support bird life to an unusual degree. In recent years the colony of terns which had lived there for generations has been threatened by gulls taking over the island's nesting places to such an extent that it has been found necessary to reduce drastically the gull population.

Access to the island is by boat from Anstruther. A Joint Committee manages the Reserve which includes a bird observatory and Field Station set up in 1947,

ANSTRUTHER

Of considerable importance in the Middle Ages as a Scottish sea-
port was the larger neighbouring village of Anstruther which nowadays
combines a straggle of hamlets some twelve miles due south of
St. Andrews. They include Anstruther Wester and Easter, with
nearby Kilrenny and Cellardyke, or Skinfasthaven as it was once
named.

Anstruther is a fishing township of much charm and character
that retains in full degree the old customs of a seafaring community.
Its mediaeval continental trade was similar to that of St. Andrews and
Crail and its townspeople once had Dutch help in building up a harbour from the surrounding marshes. This was achieved thanks to
the skill of the dyke builders from Holland in that specialised work.
The name ' Anstruther ' in fact, is claimed to mean ' head of the
marches.'

As guardian port of the Forth from the constant forays of
Scandinavians and English freebooters, the village bred a steady
supply of hardy sailors, and in the days of Nelson and earlier it was a
regular target of the press gangs. A Spanish galleon of the ill-fated
Armada sought refuge there and its crew were given a kindly welcome, thanks to the intervention of the learned minister, James
Melville, then occupant of the church of Kilrenny. It was fortunate
for the crew that Melville had decided in 1588 to give up his Chair of
Divinity at St. Mary's College in favour of the more financially re-
warding life of a parish minister. With the large family he had to
maintain he settled at Kilrenny and his linguistic abilities provided
the essential liaison when the swarthy visaged Spaniards hove to
apprehensively off ' Enster ' as it has always been known to its nat-
ives. Melville found a common language with Jan Gomez de Medini,
the Spanish admiral, and persuaded the suspicious villagers to make
them welcome. Of de Medini's flotilla of twenty galleons, all but one
had been wrecked at sea, and the remaining crew sought nothing more
than peace.

Later, de Medini was able to return their kindness when he came
to the rescue of an Anstruther vessel's crew shipwrecked off Spain.
His intercession ensured them kindly treatment and may even have
saved their lives.

Another much later sailor of note who paid a visit, but very much
unwelcome, was the notorious John Paul Jones, the Scotsman who

became an American admiral and who was only prevented from burning all the shipping in the Forth by a sudden westerly gale. Jones' small fleet was lying off Pittenweem at the time, 1779. Sir John Anstruther, the burgh's ancestral laird .... the family connection with the village dates from 1123—mistook them for ships he was expecting back from an African expedition. He sent out a boat, with newspapers and a basket of fruit and vegetables. Some local dignitaries took the opportunity of a jaunt out to the ships, but only one man was allowed on board by Jones, and he was kept there. This was Andrew Paton, a Pittenweem pilot. He was well-treated by his hosts and was landed safely in Holland after the pirate's unsuccessful foray that had the countryside in a ferment.

A ballad of the time declared :—

" Sir John went to see
What ships they might be
With a basket of fruit and the news, man.
They sent back the boat, with powder and shot,
And bade him defend Elie House, man."

(Elie House at that time was the principal residence of the Anstruther family).

Two modern hotels in the village have assumed historical names. ' The Craw's Nest ' recalls a visit by Charles II. When entertained by Sir Philip Anstruther, he drily remarked : " Such a fine supper I have gotten in a craw's nest ! " a slighting reference to the unassuming architecture of ancient Dreel Castle, the oldest part of which was built by the first Anstruther, a Norman baron, Wm. de Candela by name. Anstruther was assumed as the family name in 1235 and the family has had many notable members. One fell at Flodden, and his grandson at Pinkie Cleugh. A later Sir James and his son both earned the favour of James VI. A noted early scion was 'Fisher Willie', Sir William of Bruce's time. He was the hero of a legendary tale of mystic intervention that saved him from death by a neighbour's treachery.

At the Smuggler's Inn, the Jacobite lairds of the district are believed to have met and plotted, and it is the case that when troops of the Young Pretender entered the village they were hospitably received.

King James VI was another royal Stuart who had many associations with Anstruther, while noted literary personalities have found

166

Ancient Church of St. Athernase, Leuchars, with its rare Norman apse.

(Photos by G. M. Cowie).

Crail's fine old Town House, dominating its main street.

(*Photo by W. M. Jack*).

The fine, award-winning restoration which now houses the Scottish Fisheries Museum at Anstruther.

it attractive, including R. L. Stevenson.   A native, William Tennant, while a clerk to his brother, made himself master of several languages. He rose to become a St. Andrews Professor of Hebrew and a leading scholar in ancient languages.   He was the author of the epic poem ' Anster Fair '.   Noted sailors have included Rear Admiral Black and Lt. Waid, the latter of whom left money in 1800 to found Waid Academy, the fine school that provides secondary education for the district.   Another noted Anstruther scholar was Dr. Thomas Chalmers who was a Professor of Divinity in St. Andrews and later in Edinburgh University.   Born in 1780 he was Principal of the Free Church of Scotland at his death in 1847.   Chalmers' house in the village is a well-restored building.

As with all the other coast villages, Anstruther attracts many artists seeking to recapture on canvas its picturesque beauty which preserves an atmosphere that is redolent of earlier times.

In the earliest days of its recorded history the Augustinians of the Roman Church founded a priory there about 1114, and as their foundation did in St. Andrews, the priory soon acquired very considerable grounds.   The ruins that stand yet near the Episcopal Church show some trace of the grand scale of the original structure. The Church of St. Adrian is the Parish Church.   The old mercat cross stands against one of its walls and the remnants of the old prison are adjacent.

Unusual to find in the isolated and rural Anstruther of the Regency days an extension of the fashion of that extravagant period for clubs of all kinds.   The Beggars' Benison of Anstruther, founded by the local lairds for foregathering together in conviviality, had 32 members at its inception.   They included the Earl of Kellie famous as ' Fiddler Tam ' and Lord Newark, with of course, an Anstruther or two.   They met in a somewhat disreputable hostelry in the Card's Wynd . . . . a rustic copy of the infamous Hellfire Club.

The Beggars' Benison continued until 1836.   At its winding up, the remaining funds were handed over for use as school prizes . . . . a highly respectable ending to a bawdy reminder of Regency excesses. It recalls another local club of an entirely different kind.   While their betters were carousing, the industrious wives of the fishermen had found another occupation to relieve the drudgery and tedium of net-baiting.   Hand-loom weaving became a prospering industry all over the Neuk for a time, and its linen became well-known.   It continued

o   167 for fully a century until the industrial revolution throttled it with its mechanisation. The weavers were quick to form their own early version of a club, or union, by initiating a benevolent society on the lines of the old Seabox Societies. Kilrenny as the centre of the industry, became the headquarters of the club. At one time practically every cottage in the area had its loom, many of them beautifully constructed, and now much sought-after antiques.

The Buckie House of Anstruther is possibly the village's most photographed feature. It is typical of many fishers' houses in different parts of Scotland for its lavish use of sea-shells, or buckies, as decoration. But here the decoration is far more extensive than most. The external walls are covered with gay designs picked out in all kinds of shells, and the treatment is extended to the interior. Most of the shells were painstakingly gathered by Alexander Batchelor, owner of the house a century ago. Nearby, on the other side of the Dreel Burn bridge, is another such house.

When, some fifty years ago, the herring shoals departed from the North Sea, the village fishermen turned their attention to white fish and shellfish, including nowadays, the once-despised shrimps. In these they now have a thriving trade. The sale of their catches at the auction market when the fleet returns daily is a feature of community life, and visitors never fail to find it a fascinating scene.

Close by they will find the Scottish Fisheries Museum in the beautifully restored St. Ayles Land which is one of the oldest property sites in any Scottish burgh, possessing a charter dating back to 1318. The museum contains a collection of items that illustrate the varied aspects of the life of a Scottish fisher family, at home as well as at sea. The many exhibits include a marine aquarium. Ayles Land has served many purposes in its long existence. In very early days it was a chapel and later, much later, it became a malt barn. It once also served as a house whose occupants were wiped out by the plague of 1645 along with many other villagers. Restorer of the building and several others in the East Neuk of which he is a native is St. Andrews architect, W. Murray Jack. He has gained a number of awards for his authentic restoration work on behalf of the National Trust in different parts of Scotland.

In Kilrenny James Melville, its famous minister, built himself a fine new manse around 1590. It still stands to-day, conspicuous and proud, a tribute to Scottish workmanship, and the home once again

168

of a minister of the Scottish church. Melville's Diary is one of the great books of its kind, and it gives an intimate account of his life at St. Andrews. It also tells a great deal about the building of his manse. Kilrenny itself has an indirect connection with two assassinations that played their part in moulding Scottish history. The manse sheltered overnight, on part of his journey, James Sharp, Archbishop of St. Andrews, who met his end on Magus Moor. A sumptuous marble memorial was afterwards erected in Holy Trinity, St. Andrews by his son. A plaster cast of that memorial is a grim relic used as a wallpiece in the watchtower of the manse which Melville once used as a study.

The hamlet is also associated with the mysterious disappearance of Cardinal Beaton's corpse after his murder in St. Andrews Castle. (p. 78). In his ' Historical Fife ' A. H. Millar says :—'' There are several notable tombs in the old churchyard of Kilrenny. A ruinous, enclosed tomb at the east end of the church was supposed to mark the grave of Cardinal Beaton, brought there by his nephew, the laird of Kilrenny who was captain of St. Andrews Castle when the assassination took place. This story is not accepted without question as there is reason to believe that the Cardinal was buried in the Priory of St. Andrews ''. Or in the grounds of the Blackfriars Monastery, as Balfour avers !

The mystery is another of the many that surround this historic part of Scotland, and one that is unlikely ever to be solved. Yet, how often is it found to be the case that such stories that persist down the years are founded on a substance of fact ? What Millar recorded in 1895 could well be true.

The Beatons of Balfour for long enough possessed the lands around Kilrenny and they built the mansion house there at the close of the seventeenth century. Rennyhill, which replaced it, remained in the family hands until 1750, was sold, but came back later once more into their possession.

Also of interest in the Kilrenny churchyard is a gravestone with the carving of an old-time ship still clearly visible although carved in the 1600's. Above the ship hovers a large seabird. Cellardyke has an interesting curio of another kind. This is the jawbone of a giant whale killed in the Arctic. William Smith, sailor and explorer of the northern seas, brought it home and used it as an archway at the back of his house.   Another lasting memorial to his name will be found on Arctic maps where Smith's Sound is recorded.

PITTENWEEM

Separated by the Dreel Burn from Anstruther is the village of Pittenweem whose name is undoubtedly connected with the word ' Uamhe ' meaning cave, the cave by the shore that is believed to have been a hermit's retreat in early times.

The history of the little burgh is linked with the priory that long ago in the early Christian era stood on the May Island, and legend has it that one of the many saints named Fillan who flit through the dim realms of pre-historic Scotland, was the hermit in question.   Yet the Patron Saint of the Burgh is Adrian who died defending the May Island monastery and is credited as being the founder of the Culdee Church in the Neuk.

To-day Pittenweem is distinguished by its picturesque harbour and its streets are brightened by many lovely old houses that are typical of the best of East Neuk architecture, of which crow-stepping and red pantiles have been features for the past three centuries. Some of these houses have been preserved by the Scottish National Trust and the restored examples that overlook the harbour are not-able.   The quiet and lovely West Shore, now being increasingly ' developed ' complements the narrow wynds and closes that lead up the incline from the harbour.   They rise with a steepness that catches the breath of the fittest.   The view at the top makes the climb well worth while.

The burgh's first royal charter was granted by David 1st and it shows the superiority of the priory, the most ancient building in Pittenweem, belonged to the monks of May.   They built it after 1318 when they abandoned May Island and retained it until all was swept away in the Reformation and the lands alienated.   The ruins reveal that the priory was once a place of considerable extent.   It was dedicated, like Crail Church, to St. Mary, although the Burgh's seal depicts St. Adrian as its patron.

In the days of witchcraft, particularly in the early seventeenth century Pittenweem gained an unenviable reputation for its persecution of witches (p. 90).

The Scottish kings of early days were frequent visitors because of Pittenweem's importance as a continental trading centre, and

170

Charles II, when he visited Anstruther, also stayed over at Pittenweem where Lord Kellie entertained him with full ceremony. It was also a shipmaster of the village who took Charles II to Fesule in France after his defeat at Worcester in 1651. His house, the Giles, is one of the excellent restorations in the village.

The village marched almost en masse against Montrose and lost the flower of its manhood at the Battle of Kilsyth, to the extent that for a time there was a shortage of sailors and fishermen to man the boats. Another historical incident with which it is closely associated led up to the Porteous Riots in Edinburgh. A plaque at the end of Routine Row marks the site of the house where an exciseman was robbed by two men, Andrew Wilson, the smuggling baker, and Robertson in 1736. Their attempted escape, while on the way to their execution after trial, was the spark that started the riots.

Wilson had been caught red-handed on a smuggling expedition by the Excise men. Along with two cronies, he impudently tried to steal back the confiscated goods. The burglars were recognised and later caught and condemned to die. One of them turned King's evidence and Wilson and Robertson were taken to Edinburgh Tolbooth. In an attempted escape from the prison an act of panic by Wilson foiled their efforts, an act for which he later made gallant amends. The condemned men, on the Sunday before their execution, were escorted to the Tolbooth Church as customary, ' to make their peace.' In the midst of the service Wilson suddenly seized both his guards and called on his companion to run for it. Aided by a sympathetic congregation Robertson managed to escape and was never traced again. Wilson himself made no attempt other than to impede his guards.

Captain Porteous of the City Guard put on eighty men to forestall any recue by the sympathetic crowd when Wilson was publicly executed. The mob turned threatening and they were fired on by the Guard. Six of them fell under a hail of bullets. Porteous was tried, in his turn, and condemned to death. When a six weeks' stay of execution was given, a suspicious mob stormed the Tolbooth and carried out summary justice on Porteous.

Reminders exist in the village of a former busy trade in the export of coal, once a flourishing Pittenweem industry that would have changed irrevocably the character of the place had economic conditions allowed it to continue.

171

Pittenweem is also well-known for its covered market where the daily catches of fish are sold, and it is the fish market that has for centuries been the hub of the local activity.

Kellie Castle, not far away from the village, is worth visiting for its architectural features and as one of the notable restorations by Sir Robert Lorimer who took up residence there. Now in the possession of the National Trust, it focuses attention on traditional Fife architecture and building craftsmanship. It is open to the public on Wednesdays and Sundays in summer.

ST. MONANCE

"We live by the sea" proclaims the proud motto of St. Monance, another of the adjacent coast villages that, like its neighbours is steeped in Scottish history. St. Monance nowadays is not only noted for its fishing boats, but for the building of them by its long-established ship-building firm. James Miller's has existed since 1717, and has moved with the times to the extent that their experience was recently enlisted for the subtle art of yacht building for racing purposes, with conspicuous success.

Much historical debate has arisen over the village name. Monamus was believed to have come to this country along with Adrian, the saint closely associated with the East Neuk. On the other hand, Skene links the village with Moinenn in the Irish calendar of saints. The ancient church of St. Mary for which St. Monance is famed has been recently restored. It is second in age in the Kingdom of Fife to that of Crail, and was built on the land of Inverrin by David II in 1369, according to the historian Keith, in gratitude for the saving of his life after his vessel was wrecked on the Lady Rock. The church replaced the original shrine that was believed to have contained the saint's relics. The Colomban missionaries were probably responsible for its foundation as a Culdee establishment, just as they were known throughout the Neuk area generally for their indefatigable evangelistic work. After the Reformation it became a Reformed parish church and was linked with the neighbouring church of Abercrombie. The inland parish name fell into disuse and the union of the two took place in 1647. The remains of the Abercrombie chapel stand in the policies of Balcaskie Castle and for a time it was used as a burial place for the Anstruthers of Balcaskie.

172

The restored interior of St. Mary's is of conspicuous beauty and interest. It includes stone vaulting over the choir and the remains of the old west doorway. An unusual, but appropriate decoration is a hanging model of a full-rigged ship of the late 1700s. A considerable earlier renovation that was effected took place in 1828.

The English army burned the church in 1544 when marching on St. Andrews which they failed to reach. Forty-five years later Stewart, Earl of Bothwell, used the church as a temporary fort.

Within the village the National Trust for Scotland has co-operated with the Local Authority to restore a group of attractive and picturesque eighteenth century houses at West Shore. At one time part of the properties was used as a burgh jail and another part as a brewery. Another scheme of restoration in East Street was undertaken along with Dundee College of Art with fine success.

Standing at the gates of the church are the ruins of Newark Castle, formerly the home of the Abercrombies, one of the many ancient families of the East Neuk. In 1649 the castle was bought by Sir David Leslie, the Scots general who fought as a royalist with notable success until Cromwell defeated him at Dunbar. Sir David was the first Lord of Newark, and a number of subsequent holders of the title lie with him in the churchyard.

Amid all the signs of its venerable past, St. Monance has developed summer facilities for the numerous tourists attracted by its rugged beauty. They include a caravan site with the panorama of the Forth on its doorstep.

ELIE AND EARLSFERRY

A few miles westwards along the firth from St. Monance is the sedately quiet holiday resort of Elie and Earlsferry. It should rightly be named ' Earlsferry and Elie ', the native will stoutly assert. Indeed Earlsferry is a royal burgh of venerable age, founded around 1225. The narrative of much earlier documents provided the foundation of a charter granted by James VI.

As to be expected of an important ancient ferry over the Forth the village contained a chapel that was also a hostelry for the very early pilgrims from the Lothians and further south on their way to the holy shrine of St. Andrew at St. Andrews.

The marauding Danes around the year 1000 took advantage of the soft harbourage to land there as part of their coastal invasion. Kincraig Point, where the beach ends and the spectacular Crag begins, contains three interesting caves, and at one of the beaches near Elie garnets have been found. The neighbouring villages of Kilconquhar and Colinsburgh are picturesque inland hamlets, both of which have many houses that have been happily restored, with Kilconquhar Castle, the home of the Earl of Lindsay nearby, and Balcarres, seat of the Earl of Crawford not far away.

The Lady's Tower east of the Harbour was a summer house. The site commemorates Lady Janet Anstruther who when she wanted to bathe at the beach, a century and more ago, sent the bellman round the streets to warn the townspeople away, so that her privacy would be undisturbed. An imperious lady with a whim of iron !

Golf has been played at Elie for over two centuries and it possesses an excellent 18-hole course which is administered by the Golf House Club. Several Scottish championships have been held on the Elie Course. The most distinguished Elie golfer is James Braid who was five times Open Champion of Britain. A big, solid man of equable temperament, he was venerated by all golfers in his day.

*   *   *   *   *   *   *   *   *

A cluster of three villages still further west than Elie illustrates the historic eminence of the eastern corner of ' the kingdom of Fife ' and its residential desirability.

First are the Largos, Upper and Lower. The latter smacks of that unmistakable atmosphere of an ancient fishing port. In former days its women were noted for their industry and their fine knitting. Possessed of a rich agricultural hinterland, its farms have always been prosperous and a staple crop for generations was flax for the village weavers. A venerable thanksgiving custom, belonging more to England than to Fife, was ' decorating the maiden ', the ingathering of the last sheaf of harvest.

Nowadays Lower Largo is a holiday resort and noted as the birthplace of Alexander Selkirk, the sailor who inspired Defoe's Robinson Crusoe, after spending four years alone on a desert island. A statue stands on the site of the house where Selkirk spent his childhood.

174

Crail Harbour with the restored Customs House, the high building in the foreground.

(Photo by G. M. Cowie).

Overlooking the harbour at St. Monance, restored buildings
in the picturesque main street.

(Photos by W. M. Jack).

The Great House at Pittenweem's ancient Priory.   Another fine
example of East Neuk restoration.

Upper Largo is best-known for its thirteenth century church and its many lovely walks around Largo Law, which has strong covenanting associations. It was this solitary eminence, dominating the landscape, that reared Sir Andrew Wood, the Scottish admiral of the fifteenth century whose ships protected the trade routes from English pirates and invaders.

*   *   *   *   *   *   *   *   *

Of the close-knit triangle of villages, Lundin Links is the most conventional, with its attractive beach and golf links. It is named after the Lundin family, said to have been founded by William the Lion, under the bar sinister. The family occupied their castle overlooking the links for centuries, but all that remains of departed glory is a lone tower.

The enigmatic Standing Stones of Lundin are a magnet for archaeologists seeking to solve their mystery now lost in the impenetrable mists of time.

Of this fascinating and intriguing area described best as the East Neuk of Fife, St. Andrews is looked to as the natural centre. Just as the university city is unique as a community in Scotland, so is its hinterland untypical of most of Lowland Scotland. The ancient forests of the East Neuk, long since denuded and converted into some of the richest agricultural soil in the country, and its age-old seafishing industry, have meant that the Neuk has ever been a prized and well-stocked national larder. As such, and with its relatively isolated geographical position, it escaped the industrialisation that followed the exploitation of Fife's coal fields.

Strategically, those natural assets attracted the early kings and the early Church. They attracted the acquisitive, questing Danes from overseas. A considerable part of Scotland's earliest history consequently was enacted here and the signs of that history are everywhere evident around. That industrial Scotland has so far passed it by is so much the better for Scotland and for the East Neuk.

Modern planning proposes it should remain a wide preservation area ; a bracing and healthy combination of country and seaside, to invigorate and stimulate the nation's industrial population and to enthrall its annual invasion of global visitors.

P

175

INDEX

177

179